MW01247175

Psychic Horizons Workbooks and Workouts

How to Read Tarot Cards Intuitively

Carole Anne Somerville

ISBN-13: 978-1544910314
ISBN-10: 1544910312

Spiritual Development Workbooks

Nurture your Mind, Body, Soul & Spirit
Tap into your Psychic Self
Build your Spiritual Muscles

"It seems that these old cards were conceived deep in the guts of human experience, at the most profound level of the human psyche. It is to this level in ourselves that they will speak."
~ Sallie Nichols

Contents:

This Workbook is devoted to helping you realise how anyone, including YOU can link with the tarot.

Do you find it hard to remember the meanings of the 78 tarot cards? –

(This book will give a simple-to-understand way to learn the meanings of all the cards)

Do you keep telling yourself you can't read the tarot because you aren't psychic enough? -

(This book will help you realise how anyone including you can link with the tarot)

Do you think you have to be gifted in order to read tarot?

(This book will take you on a fascinating learning journey into the psychological and spiritual associations of the cards and will prove you don't have to be gifted to read tarot cards)

Do you want to start reading tarot for yourself and your friends?

(This book will teach you the traditional tarot card meanings and also intuitive tarot card meanings.)

How does it work?

* All you need is a deck of tarot cards.

* This book will include exercises, meditations or questions for you to answer.

* You will work through these, keeping a note of your responses in your tarot journal.

* Once you have read and completed the exercises in this book, you will have a good understanding of the traditional and

intuitive meanings of the tarot cards and the confidence to read the tarot for yourself and others.

I would recommend that you start a Journal before you begin reading this book in which you can record results of exercises, dreams and intuitive experiences.

I hope you will enjoy this fun and insightful journey.

One
An introduction to the tarot

The Structure of a Tarot Deck; becoming familiar with your
Tarot Deck and Images on the Cards

There are many ways to learn the tarot. Every card has its
traditional meaning but learning the keywords of each card
can seem daunting to the beginner. Learning how to use these
keywords while also trying to understand how to read a tarot
card spread might seem almost impossible to some. This can
cause people to feel they will never understand the tarot.
 It is true that each card in the tarot has its traditional
interpretation. However through this book you will discover
that the deeper meanings within the tarot come through
symbols on the cards. Symbols are the "language of the soul".
We see symbols in our dreams. – Images, colours, words and
numbers can all convey a spiritual meaning and in this book
I'm going to help you understand how to read the images on
tarot cards by allowing the symbols to trigger an intuitive
response within you.
 So the real meaning will come intuitively as the cards begin to
speak to you. – Don't worry if you feel you aren't psychic or
intuitive and you will never be able to read the tarot
intuitively. Exercises and meditations in this book will help
you tap into your intuitive side which if not used regularly can
become suppressed. Like all skills and talents, the more we use
them the better we get at it. If they are ignored, they will
become rusty. Through this book, you will start to develop and
use your sixth sense to read tarot cards.
 The tarot deck used in this book will be the Rider Waite deck,
however, you should use a deck that you feel drawn to. The
meanings associated with the Rider Waite deck can be easily
transferred to any other standard deck of tarot cards. There
are many oracle cards available on-line. A standard tarot deck
will include 22 major arcana cards and 56 minor arcana cards.

Included in this book will be:
 * A guide to learning the meanings of all 78 tarot cards
 * An introduction to reversed cards and how to apply these in your readings
 * A guide to tarot card spreads and how to interpret cards in a spread
 * A guide to understanding the elements, numerology and astrology in the tarot
 * Exercises, meditations and sample responses for each lesson to help you in your learning

The tarot can offer insight into your situation at a given time. Tarot cards do not foretell events that will definitely occur, "no matter what". We all have our own free will ... the ability to make choices. ... The freedom to choose – along with the constraints imposed on us by circumstance, time and relationships – all suggests that everything is interdependent. What the tarot reflects is situations, experiences and trends we are going through on our journey through life.
 The tarot can also suggest trends and cycles we are experiencing. Due to circumstances, outside influences and unexpected change even, there are events that will inevitably happen that we have no control over. These pre-ordained events are what is meant by Fate.

We all go through phases and cycles during our life's journey. We also see cycles around us every day:
 * day turns to night
 * the Moon's phases from New Moon symbolic of birth and new starts to Full Moon representing endings and completion
 * the seasons: spring, summer, autumn and winter
 * time and calendar cycles
 * astronomical cycles
 * agricultural cycles

Life too, can be viewed as a series of cycles.

Tarot cards reflect those cycles and if this can help us to recognise which part of the cycle we are currently going through, this makes it easier for us to understand what preparations are necessary for the next phase of that cycle.

Images in the Tarot

Images on each tarot card can be admired consciously as works of art but they will also touch the reader on a deeper subconscious level. These images will trigger feelings (they might for instance make us feel hopeful, happy or sad). Each card holds symbolic images that serve to convey a meaning to the reader. Studying the illustrations and symbols will help you understand the meaning of each tarot card. Traditional meanings will be given in this book but you will also be encouraged to use your intuition to read the cards too. As you read the tarot remember that you cannot be wrong. Whatever meaning springs to mind is right for you even if it isn't what the books might say. Images and symbols also contain links with other branches of divination such as astrology and numerology as you will discover later in this book.

Your Tarot Deck

There are 78 cards in a tarot deck. 22 in the Major Arcana, 16 court cards and 40 numbered cards in each of the four suits: pentacles, cups, swords and wands.

The word 'Arcana' means secrets or mysteries. The Major Arcana represent significant life events so the more Major Arcana cards there are in a spread the more likely it is that the person you are reading for is going through an important phase in life. Each of the Major Arcana cards is numbered and follows a sequence of stages from 0 the Fool, the beginning to 21 the World and completion.

The Minor Arcana consists of 56 cards divided into four suits: Wands, Cups, Pentacles and Swords. There are ten numbered cards in each suit and four court cards, usually called the Page, Knight, Queen and King.

There are numerous decks available. Some are quite old in their design but many are modern, their illustrations and symbols inspired by many diverse subjects and ideas. Whatever deck you are using, the method for reading the cards is the same and this book will help you explore the meanings of your tarot cards.

Images on each card act as a visual clue to the meaning and this can trigger feelings, emotions, words and images of your own that will help you read the card. The best way to learn how to read the tarot is not by rote and key words but to learn to feel what each card is saying to you.

All symbols, letters, numbers, colours, scenes and activity in a tarot card image is telling you something meaningful. As you see the image this will stir up your thoughts and feelings and bring an intuitive response. This is how your cards speak to you. Although we will be looking at every individual card, here are just some of the ways you might consider the images in the cards.

NUMBERS – Most tarot cards have numbers. As well as indicating the card's place in the tarot deck, these numbers have a special meaning of their own.

WORDS – Some tarot cards will have their name written on the card. Not only is this an indication of which card it is, the actual word can trigger all sorts of images in our minds. What for instance do you think of, the moment you see the name 'Hermit'? Or 'the World'?

PEOPLE – Some tarot cards contain images of people. These might relate to an aspect of your personality or your current role in life (the Empress for instance might suggest you are a caring, loving person with a nurturing personality or seeds are being sown. – Something new is beginning and this can be anything from a creative idea, a new relationship to a new life). Or this card can relate to someone in your life who cares about you in a motherly way.

ACTIONS – Most people in the tarot card images will be doing something specific and this will give you a clue to the card's meaning.

MAIN SCENE – The main scene in the tarot card is where a lot of the symbolism can be found. What is happening in the card? Which colour is predominant? How does the overall image make you feel?

OBJECTS – There are often objects in each card. These might be cups, wands, swords or pentacles but also flowers, trees, crowns, thrones, streams, mountains ... each of these objects will have a specific meaning.

ELEMENTS – The four elements mainly featured in tarot cards are Fire, Earth, Air and Water and all of these have symbolic meanings. The elements can also be linked with the astrology signs which can also be grouped into elements.

How do you bond with your tarot deck?

Treat your tarot deck like a friend. Respect your cards. You might keep them in a wooden box wrapped in silk or a nice cloth but this is entirely up to you. I have a number of decks kept in boxes but others I keep in the box they came in. You might have a special place to keep your tarot cards.

You don't have to sleep with your cards under your pillow to bond with them, although some people do and if this feels right for you, go ahead and do it. You don't have to carry your cards around with you to form a bond with them but again if that's what you want to do, trust your instincts. What you can do, to acquaint yourself with your cards, is to shuffle them well, then look at each card one at a time. Start to get familiar with the imagery on the cards.

Who you want to touch your cards is also an important consideration. – We all give off our own energy vibrations. A loving personality for instance has a light vibration with a high frequency. Conversely, someone who is often angry and resentful will have a heavy vibration and low frequency. To bond with your deck, touch your cards regularly and you will be charging them with your energy. You might prefer that other people don't touch your cards or the energy could get confused. Or, if like me, you may not mind that your family touches your cards because their destiny is already linked with your own.

Can tarot cards predict the future? –

The future is not written in stone. Tarot cards, like astrology and other methods of divination can suggest possible trends we are going through in life and what may happen if we continue to follow a certain path. We all have free will and can make our own decisions. Tarot cards can offer us guidance on how we might choose different paths or different directions. Tarot cards help give insight into what is going on and what we are feeling and experiencing in our life and relationships to help give us a better understanding of what we are going through.

Before going any further, I want to cover a few things you may have heard about the tarot: questions people often bring up when they first start on this amazing learning journey.

- You have to be psychic to read the tarot – you don't. Anyone can read the tarot. Even if you use interpretations from out of a book, the tarot cards will speak to you and often this is how beginners start reading tarot cards.

- Your tarot deck should be received as a gift – it used to be said that you should not buy your own tarot deck but it should be given to you as a gift (some people will still tell you this). This is not true. There are many tarot decks available. You might feel drawn to more than one deck. Don't wait for someone to buy this for you. There is nothing wrong with purchasing it for yourself. If you still feel a little superstitious about this, you might look on it as a gift to yourself!
- Tarot cards cause things to happen – they don't. Tarot cards are like looking into a mirror. They reflect what is going on within yourself or within your life at the time you consult them.
- Tarot cards should be wrapped in silk and kept in a wooden box – I keep some of my cards in silk and in wooden boxes but others in the box they came in. All work fine for me. Even so there is something about the ritual of opening the box and unwrapping the silk that helps form the right mood for a tarot card reading. You should go with what works for you.
- You have to be in a room with a tarot reader to get a reading – not true. I have done many hundreds of on-line readings through tuning into a photograph or a name with feedback that proves that I have made a good connection with the person I was reading for. We tune into the energy of the person who requests a reading whether they are in the room with us or are thousands of miles away. All that is required is that the person has asked for the reading and has given permission for you to read for them.
- Tarot cards can be used as a tool to develop your intuition – true.

Your Tarot Journal

To begin this book you will need to keep a tarot journal. This can be a book or an on-line journal.

Starting your Tarot Journey

For the first exercise in this book, you will be looking at the illustrations on each card. Remember there are no right or wrong answers. The purpose of this exercise is to help you familiarise yourself with the images on your cards. A deeper look at the meanings of each card will come later on in the book. As you do this exercise, just go with the flow and above all: enjoy.

Tarot Tips

Spend time holding your tarot deck and looking at the cards. Try to form a bond with your tarot cards and treat them like an old friend. You will be amazed how quickly your tarot cards will start to speak to you.

Try to work with your tarot cards every day, even for just a few minutes. The more you hold your deck and become familiar with the illustrations on the cards, the faster the learning process will be.

There is no right or wrong way to read the tarot. When working with your cards, however you choose to read them is right for you.

Tarot Toolbox

Exercise 1

You will be learning the meanings of the tarot cards through the lessons in this book. Here are seven daily exercises to help you bond with your cards and become familiar with their illustrations.

On the first day shuffle your cards. Now deal 11 cards onto a table face down. From this pile turn over the top card and look at it. In your journal write down the name of the card. Now spend about one minute looking at the card. Ask yourself: how do you feel when you see the images in this card? What do you think it is telling you? Are there any people in the card? If so, what are they doing? Do they look happy or sad? Are they standing still, moving away from or approaching a place? Are they calm or do they look nervous?

When you are ready, write down the feeling this card gives you and what you think this card means. Do the same with the next ten cards. Now carefully put this pile of 11 cards face upwards at the bottom of your deck of cards.

On the second day (don't shuffle your cards) just deal another 11 cards from the top of your pile onto the table face down. Repeat day one's exercise with these cards, making a note in your journal of how you feel when you look at each card and what you think is the meaning of the card.

Continue this over the next five days until you have worked through your whole deck. – Response from our students to this exercise will be included at the back of this book.

Two
The Major Arcana

Recognising the Major Arcana Cards and Understanding how the Major Arcana represents important stages in Life's Journey

Cards belonging to the Major Arcana are the movers-and-shakers of the tarot. There are 22 cards in the Major Arcana and these cards represent the lessons we all learn as we journey through life.

Many of these cards place emphasis on our inner self: what drives us, our emotions and feelings, our motivations, hopes, reactions and psychic development rather than external life events. When they do represent something going on in our life, it's usually quite major.

A predominance of Major Arcana cards in a reading suggests that what the sitter is currently going through or the issues on their mind are extremely significant. These cards can also be used on their own for tarot readings about important life issues.

Although the future isn't written in stone, our life goes through a series of important cycles and the Major Arcana cards, like the outer planets in astrology, reveal trends or cycles that are occurring at the time of the reading. These are therefore cards of destiny and yes we all have our own free will but what these cards reveal is likely to happen or will occur. – Either within ourselves or on the outside. – These experiences, if approached in a philosophical way, can be seen as lessons we have to go through and learn from.

The Major Arcana cards are numbered from 0 – the Fool to 21 – the World. There are 22 cards in all. Each card tells a story and these cards in themselves from 0 to 21 represent one whole cycle and a series of smaller cycles within this cycle from the beginning (the Fool) to completion (the World).

There are many references to the Fool's journey through the Major Arcana and these cards can be grouped together in a few ways from innocence to enlightenment or according to groups of People, Concepts, Changes and Qualities. To try to make it easier for you to learn, we will focus on two groups: the first eleven (cards 1 to 10) and the next eleven (cards 11 to 21). Ending with the World at 21.

So from 0, the beginning, with the Fool, it is helpful to see yourself as the Fool and each card he meets is a destination along his journey. In an actual reading, all cards can relate to the sitter (the person the reading is for).

The following description of the first half of the Fool's journey through the Major Arcana is based on the Rider Waite cards. However, it doesn't matter if your deck is Shadowscapes, the Robin Wood Tarot or the Deck of the Cats, as long as they are tarot cards, this will work just as well for them too.

While following this journey, deal out your Major Arcana cards in the following way. At the top place the Fool. Now deal two rows with 1 to 10 on the top row with 11 to 21 lined up directly underneath these.

This will pair the cards together and although each pair isn't perfectly related, some similarities will be seen between them. Underneath these cards, place the World.

The Fool's Journey

So let's take the top row first.

0 the Fool can be male or female. This card represents the start of a journey into the unknown. Although the word 'fool' might conjure up images of a medieval jester – a professional clown employed to entertain a king or nobleman – this man is no fool.

(Even in medieval times in being given leeway to say anything in 'jest' the Fool was sometimes the only member of court who was able to voice an honest opinion about the plight of the king's subjects. Through using wit they were sometimes able to persuade the king to take action to help the local community.)

Our Fool is innocent, filled with excitement and hope for the future, his foot is upraised as he is heading off a cliff (ready to step into the unknown). At his feet a little dog is trying to warn him of the danger ahead.

All cycles need a beginning and the Fool represents the start of a new cycle. The Fool steps into the unknown, in innocence or ignorance or both. He has no baggage. – Just a small bag on a staff resembling a wand. His nature is full of playful surprises, carefree and unpredictable. The zero suggests this is just before the journey begins. Nothing yet has begun. This card can represent new starts or a change of direction. If intuitively you sense it is time for a change, the Fool tells you to trust your instincts. Take a leap of faith. Follow your heart.

Step 1 the Fool meets the Magician, his spiritual guide. The Magician has skills and knowledge he can draw on in his future journey.

The Magician has all the skills necessary (see on the table in front of him, a cup, wand, pentacle and sword) to develop the Fool's skills and nurture his creativity. The Magician can bring an opportunity to achieve but also a need to act quickly or the opportunity will pass us by. The Magician can also manipulate in order to get things to go his own way.

Step 2 the Fool meets the High Priestess, mistress of mystical and metaphysical power. While the Magician is the master of physical power, the High Priestess introduces the Fool to his spiritual side. She represents spiritual growth, intuition and the power of the subconscious. She can put the Fool in touch with his intuitive side through dreams and through sudden flashes of intuition or inspiration. She will not manipulate like the Magician. She uses her power to teach and guide. Whenever you need to listen to your inner voice, the High Priestess will come up in a spread. The Magician and the High Priestess are the first paired cards in the Major Arcana representing the material and the spiritual world, the conscious and unconscious mind. At the beginning of any journey, the first thing we become aware of is that we 'are' in a physical sense and we exist also within ourselves too.

Step 3 the Fool meets the Empress, a creative, loving and fertile woman. The Empress is goddess of nature and associated with Venus, goddess of love and beauty. The Fool hasn't yet encountered love, affection and comfort. These are qualities the Empress brings into his life. She can be a motherly influence or a loving, supportive partner. The Empress teaches the Fool how to love and care for himself and how to care for others and respect nature. When the Empress appears in a spread, she is reminding you of physical pleasures: appreciating nature, being creative, enjoying loving relationships. She puts you in touch with your earthy feelings.

Step 4 the Fool meets the Emperor. This card pairs with the Empress. He represents masculine power. Just as the Empress is the mother, the Emperor is the loving father. He is strict, yet compassionate and although not as emotional as the Empress, he still has a strong ability to love and guide. The Emperor is a man of authority, driven to succeed. While the Empress (mother figure) protects the Fool, the Emperor (father figure) will guide him and teach him how to persevere, solve problems and achieve through determination.

So far the Fool's journey has gone through Self and meeting his parents. Now he must step outside the family and into the outside world.

Step 5 the Fool meets the Hierophant. He represents a religious leader, teacher or mentor and tradition. The lessons he can give the Fool are necessary for his development. The Fool might stop on his journey at the Hierophant, to learn from or listen to the messages that he gives. Whether he accepts or rejects them will be up to the Fool. Following tradition and having structure in your life can help you gain new levels of understanding. It can be valuable to allow a mentor or someone else to take the driving seat for a short while. But acknowledging too that tradition and past conditioning can be restraining can be the first challenge the Fool faces. The Fool who pushes through tradition rather than surrendering to the dictates of religious or cultural beliefs is the Fool who creates his own path. – Remember that this card is not all about religion as some people believe but also represents cultural traditions, social conditioning and conformity to society.

Step 6 the Fool meets the Lovers. This card isn't necessarily about love. When the Fool meets the Lovers he is encountering the first of many choices he will make in his life. It can represent a choice between two lovers or two possibilities.

This is a time when the Fool ceases to be so focused on himself and starts looking for relationships. Of course when the Lovers appear in a spread this doesn't mean it's the first time the sitter has made a choice. Someone new may have entered their life and the choice might involve considering what happens to existing relationships, routines and preferences when new energies come into their world. This card represents a critical life decision. A crossroads has been reached and there must be a choice between two paths. Once the choice is made, there will be no going back.

Step 7 the Fool meets the Chariot and this card offers the Fool the chance to take control of his own destiny. The Chariot represents self-discipline and willpower. This card shows movement and it can sometimes be a little scary when life moves forward. The Fool needs to take control of the reins to take control of his life and his destiny. In a spread, this card can suggest triumph over obstacles, a strong sense of direction and the ability to make use of past experience, knowledge and lessons learned to move forward.

Step 8 the Fool meets Strength. This card is often paired with the Chariot, representing inner strength and self-control (as the Chariot represents outer strength) and wisdom. The Fool may be facing up to his inner demons or discovering parts of himself he previously didn't know was there. This is the kind of strength that will help overcome life's obstacles or his inner-beast. When this card appears in a reading it suggests the sitter should face their inner fears, control their emotions and learn how to use their inner strength wisely. – They can and will get through a challenging situation but through using quiet strength rather than outward force.

Steps six, seven and eight describe the Fool's dealings with the outside world. In the next card he will be withdrawing, into himself.

Step 9 the Fool meets the Hermit. Having found the strength to deal with adversity, the Fool now is ready to withdraw from society to search for inner-truth. Answers will now come from within. It can be good to spend time alone in order to gather thoughts, consider new ideas and to seek inner guidance. Shining the light inside himself, the Fool is able to seek guidance from within. He can only do this in isolation. Wisdom can be gained through meditation, analysing dreams, relaxing to music, spiritual development, religion, reading, writing or counselling. Time alone can be a great way to gain enlightenment but when taken to extremes and literally becoming a hermit, it can block further progress. This card also indicates that the sitter should be willing to share their wisdom as through understanding their own experiences, they are in a better position to give advice to others.

Step 10 the Fool jumps aboard the Wheel of Fortune. This is the first card in the Major Arcana which brings change and situations over which the Fool has no control. The wheel is ever turning and as the Fool is on the wheel, will it take him to the top, towards new experiences that fill him with hope and excitement, or will it take him downwards, bringing changes that aren't so welcome. Some things just happen. They might seem to happen by chance but the Fool will eventually acknowledge that whatever the experience, it was meant to be. Because in order to appreciate the great times, he must experience the difficult times too. The Universe has an inherent harmony. The Wheel of Fortune is ever turning taking the Fool through the highs and the lows of life's journey. The Fool will learn to make the most of the highs and how to cope with the lows.

The Next path of the Fool's Journey: the Fool is now entering the second row of cards you have dealt and although the pairing isn't perfect, there are similarities in the pairs that might help you remember what each card means.

Step 11 the Fool meets Justice. Experiences in this stage of the Fool's life will help him relate to the need for Justice. This card is more representative of divine justice rather than man's justice (as all humans, no matter how fair they try to be can allow bias to colour their thinking even if they don't realise this is happening). This card represents a fair, impartial and balanced judge. When it appears in a spread it recommends that decisions and choices should be weighed very carefully. This card brings consequences of past actions. It also suggests a need for balance and harmony. When reversed, this card has similarities with the Magician reversed: both reversed cards suggesting that someone is making decisions or taking action from a prejudiced point of view and, in the case of the Magician is manipulating a situation for their own benefit. When Justice turns up in a spread, it is time for a moral inventory. This card suggests the Fool should look back over his recent past, take responsibility for his actions and decisions and use this to determine what his next move should be.

Step 12 the Fool meets the Hanged Man. At first the Fool finds it strange to come across a man hanging upside down from a tree but he has no cause for alarm. The man seems quite willing to be there. He has made it his choice to be in this position for a reason because in looking at the world upside down he is seeing it from a different perspective. This stage in the fool's journey seems to bring a pause ... life has slowed down ... he is starting to feel that he is in limbo. This makes the Fool who has so far accepted all responsibilities and commitments given to him without question, to realise too that there are aspects of his own life that are weighing heavily upon him and he is starting to feel drained and weary by it all. Some of these experiences have been painful and although it is difficult to let go, he realises that until he does, they will always hang over him like a dark shadow. It is time to let go of aspects of the past and life will start to flow again, more smoothly. Through looking at life from a different angle, the Fool has found a new perspective.

How can this card be paired with the High Priestess? The High Priestess prompts us to look for answers within. To seek guidance from a different perspective: from our dreams, meditations and our intuition. The Hanged man encourages us to look at our situation from a different perspective. Both reflections will bring fresh insight and suddenly everything will seem to make more sense.

Step 13 the Fool meets Death. This card brings transformation. It is no accident that it falls immediately after the Hanged Man. The Fool has outgrown some beliefs or has experienced all he can from certain aspects of his life and it is time for them to end in order to make room for new beginnings. These endings aren't always easy. It can be difficult to say goodbye to what has been familiar. Transition can be painful. But the Fool will come to realise that these experiences can be an opening to some amazing life experiences.

How can this card be paired with The Empress? Death can relate to new beginnings: a new baby, a new relationship, a new chapter. The Empress too relates to birth (the birth of new creative projects, birth of a baby, seeds being sown). When I first started learning the tarot I was pregnant with my first child. My spread contained the Death card. Ignorant at the time to what this meant, it scared me so much that I gave the cards to my sister (an insightful tarot reader) and said I didn't want to see them again. She explained what Death meant but I still didn't want the cards back. Years later as I became more understanding of the tarot I realised the card was so appropriate for that phase of my life: birth was a time of transition. My old way of life was ending and new beginnings: the start of my family, approaching.

Step 14 the Fool meets Temperance. The Fool has now experienced many ups and downs and has been through a number of challenges and difficulties.

As the Fool meets Temperance he realises the need for moderation and self-restraint. Temperance can bring a time of 'waiting' in which case the Fool might use this wisely, taking advantage of a peaceful episode to regain his energy. Temperance relates to equilibrium and moderation.

How can Temperance be paired with the Emperor? The Emperor is in control of his emotions. He advocates structure and order. Patience will bring just rewards. Temperance also suggests the need for patience. Temperance encourages moderation and balance. Some events might occur which knock our emotional equilibrium out of kilter, bringing the need to control our feelings and to get a sense of self again ... the sense of 'self' represented by the Emperor.

Step 15 the Fool meets the Devil. The Fool, in his craving for different experiences, finds himself in a situation where he is bound to someone or something. He entered this willingly. There is nothing keeping him tied to the situation and he can leave whenever he desires. But sometimes willpower is not strong when the Fool is having fun. He might be aware of his other responsibilities but he is enjoying himself too much to be too bothered about it. Or he may be in a work situation where his boss is pulling the strings. The Fool gets on with his work willingly but eventually he starts feeling as if there should be more to life than to allow someone else to have so much control over him. When the Devil appears in a spread it can suggest that an obsession, addiction, material-attachment, strong passions, negative thought patterns or co-dependency might be hindering personal growth and development. Any of these inner-demons can lead to a feeling of being 'controlled' rather than of 'having control'. The sitter may feel trapped in a situation but there is a way out. The chains that bind are an illusion. There is always a choice to break away ... look for choices you have been too blind to see.

How can the Devil be paired with the Hierophant, card number 5? The Hierophant signifies communication with our higher self; consciously learning, studying, taking an interest in religious or academic subjects. In this second cycle of the tarot, the Devil represents our inner-demons, negative habits and behavioural patterns. The Hierophant can indicate ties to social norms or beliefs instilled in childhood that have no real meaning anymore, that keep a person constrained until they break free. The Devil indicates ties to unhealthy relationships, bad habits, addictive patterns until the person can break free. In both instances it is possible to break free of restrictions with willpower.

Step 16 the Fool meets the Tower. The Tower brings events that make it feel as if the Fool's life is falling apart. All that he has built so far seems like it is crumbling down around him. This will be a rapid change, like a lightning strike, happening suddenly and unexpectedly. The change may happen within (a sudden realisation that beliefs instilled in childhood aren't meaningful for instance and this will change your whole way of thinking) or on the outside. It is a change that cannot be avoided. There is a sense of hope in this card too as once the dust settles at the bottom, the Fool can rebuild and start over.

How can the Tower be paired with the Lovers? The Lovers brings a situation in which choices must be made. A situation over which some people feel they have no control. Having to make a choice can cause some people a lot of stress. The indecision makes a situation more tense and traumatic. The choice can bring great change: an overworked businessman standing at a crossroads wondering whether to continue working all hours and risk losing his marriage or does he spend more time with his family? Either choice would bring a big change in life, in routines and in finances. The Tower causes disruption; choices indicated by the Lovers too can cause disruption although this will not be as drastic as the Tower.

Step 17 the Fool meets the Star. Once through the storm caused by the Tower and the dust has settled, the Fool encounters a promise of renewal ... a fresh beginning. The Star brings a feeling of renewed hope, expectation, illumination and harmony. The Star tells the Fool to accept all help that is offered. He should pay attention to his intuition. The Fool should trust that all will be well and be ready to share his joy with the world.

How can the Star be paired with the Chariot? These cards, numbered 7 and 17 are closely connected. In the Rider Waite cards notice how the rider of the chariot is wearing a crown of the same stars that are in the Star card. If these two cards appear in a reading, a vision (represented by the Star) will manifest into worldly success (Chariot).

Step 18 the Fool meets the Moon. The Fool has had many journeys, both physical, emotional and spiritual and he encounters the Moon as he goes inside himself. As his thoughts wander off into a world of their own he gets caught up in imagination and fantasy and encounters the Moon. He starts to realise that he can be very intuitive, creative and imaginative. That there is so much going on within himself that he hasn't yet realised. Digging deeper and he could discover secrets from his past, memories he has been supressing. These might come to him in his dreams. Has he been deceiving himself or has someone been deceiving him? If there has been deception, the Moon will illuminate this.

How can the Moon be paired with Strength? Strength represents 'inner strength' an inner determination that can bring success without the need for outer aggression or forcefulness. Inner strength is built up through a balance of subconscious drives and higher thinking. The Lion is symbolic of our deepest emotions.

He dwells in the realm of our unconscious (represented by the Moon). The Moon also highlights inner awareness, intuition and the subconscious. The Moon relates to our primitive urges as Strength relates to our higher self.

Step 19 the Fool meets the Sun. The Sun shines bright in the Fool's world now. The Fool closes his eyes and feels the warmth of the Sun energising his body and soul. The Sun can bring a reason for celebration. New hope, prosperity, happiness, pregnancy, a gift, joyful family moments, a holiday, wonderful friendships and happy relationships. The Sun brings happy experiences.

How can the Sun be paired with the Hermit? The Hermit is a card of looking deep into ourselves to get in touch with our intuition and spiritual side bringing about personal spiritual growth. The Sun is a card of personal growth and getting to know ourselves through our relationships.

Step 20 the Fool meets Judgement. Almost at the end of the journey, Judgement brings a milestone in the Fool's life. The Fool is reaching the end of a phase and this is a perfect opportunity to look back and assess how he has done. This will help him make decisions that are necessary for his future. Judgement calls for the Fool to sort things through in his mind. This card can bring a transition; a rebirth; a time to move on. It is a good time to start on a new chapter in life, to follow new dreams and visions. This card can also relate to legal matters and decisions.

How can Judgement be paired with the Wheel of Fortune? Both Judgement and the Wheel of Fortune are cards of Karma and Destiny. Both will bring change according to our past actions ... we reap what we sow.

Step 21 the Fool meets the World. There is a sense of completion. The Fool has gone as far as he can go on this journey. It is complete. It has brought new levels of understanding and success. The Fool will never stop growing. He is ready now to begin on fresh experiences and to start on a new life cycle. He is no longer an innocent Fool but rather a Hero who has accomplished much. He is ready now to embark on new journeys.

****

For your Tarot Journal:

The following fun exercise can be done in your journal. It involves questions relating to each card in the Major Arcana. These questions relate to personal matters and are therefore designed for you as a way to consider how these cards might relate to your life.

As you consider these questions, write down the thoughts and feelings that come to you.

The Fool

Is there a time in your life when you trusted your intuition, threw caution to the wind and leaped into a situation with no thought to the possible consequences? If so what happened?

The Magician

What skills are you proud of? Which skills are you using at this time in your life?

Sorceress/High Priestess

Can you remember your last dream? How might you analyse it?

Empress

When was the last time you pampered yourself? How often do you visit the countryside and feel in touch with nature?

Emperor

What are your current aims? What achievements do you feel most proud of?

Hierophant/Sage

Is there a teacher you can remember as having inspired you? How would you describe your spiritual/religious beliefs?

The Lovers

Was there a time when you had to make a choice from two distinct options? Which choice did you make? Do you feel it was the right one?

The Chariot/Challenge

When have you needed to be brave and face up to your fears? What did it feel like afterwards?

Justice

Do you see injustice in the world around you? What can you do to change it? If you are unable to do this, why?

The Hermit

Do you meditate regularly? Do you make time just for yourself? Do you enjoy your own company?

The Wheel/Karma

Can you remember a time when life was changing and you had no control over this? Did you fight it or go with the flow? Was it change for the better?

Strength

Can you remember a time when you had to find inner strength to cope with outer situations? Or when you had to make personal sacrifices to be strong for someone else?

Hanged Man/Reflection

Are there any views or opinions you have had which, on reflection, you have realised were completely wrong?

Death

Has there been a time when you underwent a complete change/transformation? When you had to let go of the past? What did this experience feel like at the time? How do you feel when you look back on it?

Temperance

Is there a part of your life that just seems to be flowing harmoniously at the moment?

The Devil

Have you ever been addicted to anything? How difficult was it to break out of this habit?

Have you ever felt in a position where you were tied to someone or something and at the time thought it was impossible to break out of it only eventually you did?

The Tower

What has been the most devastating experience you have ever lived through? How has this experience affected you? Has it made you stronger?

The Star

What are your current hopes? Are you grateful for your blessings? Name some.

The Moon

How do you feel your subconscious speaks to you? Are you in tune with your subconscious? Can you trust your intuition? Is there a side to yourself you keep hidden from others?

The Sun

When was the last time you had cause for a family or personal celebration? Can you recall a holiday or special moments when you felt truly relaxed and happy?

Judgment/Liberation

Have you made mistakes and owned up to it? Have you ever been through a legal battle? What were the consequences? Do you feel they were fair?

The World

What was your favourite holiday? Do you enjoy travel (in mind or physically) and finding out about the world? Can you recall a time when you reached the end of a phase and had reason to feel proud of yourself?

****

Major Arcana Tarot Exercise

You can think of your own keywords to go with each card and add these to your tarot journal. For this exercise, can you think of any books, song or movie associations that you feel relate to the Cards in the Major Arcana? I will include feedback we have received from our students on this exercise and others, at the end of this book.

Three
Symbolism in the Tarot

Understanding the use of Symbolism in the Tarot and the meaning of the Common Symbols in the cards

Symbolism in the Images in the Tarot

What was your favourite holiday? Do you enjoy travel (in mind or physically) and finding out about the world? Can you recall an experience that changed your life? The beautiful images in tarot cards subtly help the reader tune into the intuitive side of their brain to receive the messages shown in the cards. Tarot, like dreams and all mystic traditions, is rich in symbolism. When reading cards we don't just 'see' but delve deeper to discover the hidden meanings behind each symbol.

To understand symbolism in the simplest form: we see symbolism all around us and will instinctively understand what some symbols are telling us. A red traffic light tells you to stop. A gold cross on a necklace can be symbolic of the wearer's religious faith. A gold band on the third finger of the left hand is symbolic of a married person. Red roses are symbolic of love. A dove, symbolic of peace. Thunder storms may be used in literature as a symbol of chaos or disaster looming.

Symbols on a tarot card help you to interpret its message. When you're doing a reading and your mind goes blank, look at a card and ask yourself: what is the first symbol that catches your eye on this card? What do you think it is telling you? If for instance your eyes are drawn to the Lion on the Strength card you might consider whether you're in a situation which needs courage? How courageous are you? Are you brave enough to protect yourself or others or are you being overly forceful? When you are drawn to certain symbols, this is not by chance.

You are intuitively being guided to the important issues in a reading.

Understanding symbolism is a big part of the learning process when reading the tarot. You can delve as deeply into the symbolism in a card as you want to.

In this lesson we will discuss common symbols in the tarot and their meanings. Consider the interpretations below but remember too, that each symbol can mean something very different to you. So, when reading your cards, think about how the symbols speak to you. The following is meant to help you understand how you might start learning to read symbols.

Symbolism in the Tarot

Angels:

(Cards: Lovers, Wheel of Fortune, Temperance, Judgement, Queen of Swords)

Most tarot decks, not just the Rider Waite tarot have a large number of angels or winged figures in their images. An Angel is a superior being; a divine messenger. Their appearance on a card can signify important information that can be gleaned from the reading for the sitter or that the sitter may receive themselves through their dreams, experiences or flashes of inspiration. An Angel can be symbolic of our subconscious or our higher mind.

Arch:

(Cards: 3 Pentacles, 10 Pentacles, 4 Wands)

Symbol of passageways or openings to step through (new perspectives to look at life from) ... new opportunities. Arches can also represent stability and support. We often see arches in spiritual buildings such as monasteries and cathedrals, symbolising strength and support.

Arches, in mythology, often represent thresholds from one world to another. Arches can also symbolise our identity within a group, receiving and giving help where it is needed.

Bird:

(Cards: Wheel of Fortune, Star, World)

Creatures of the air, birds can symbolise freedom, high ideals, matters of the spirit. Birds can be symbolic of the human soul, representing joy, goodness and wisdom.

Bridges:

(Cards: 5 Cups)

Bridges can be a link between two worlds. Bridges can be symbolic of progress or crossing ... overcoming hardship. A bridge offers the opportunity to cross from one place or path to another. An inner knowing that 'change is needed'.

Chains:

(Card: The Devil)

Chains in the tarot are symbolic of restricting situations that have been entered into willingly or self-imposed restrictions. Chains can represent dependence ... to habits, addictions, a relationship. Chains can also give feelings of security as they impose a limit that cannot be over-stepped.

Children:

(Sun, 6 Cups, 10 Cups, 6 Swords, 10 Pentacles)

Children in the tarot can be symbolic of hope, happiness and new beginnings.

Clouds:

(Lovers, Judgement, Tower, Wheel of Fortune, Ace of Swords, 3 Swords, 5 Swords, Page Swords, King Swords, Ace cups, 4 Cups, 7 Cups, Ace Wands, Ace Pentacles)

Clouds can blow quickly across the sky without bringing any rain or they can be a sign of a storm coming. Clouds can signify an idea, message or happening that seems to come out of nowhere. They can also symbolise revelation. Clouds can be symbolic of casting a shadow over an issue. They can represent a psychic veil that can be (transcended)/ Bright clouds can be symbolic of feelings of hope and optimism. Dark clouds can be symbolic of pessimism and depression.

Dog:

(The Fool, Moon, 10 Pentacles)

Dogs can represent loyalty, guidance, protection, faithfulness, watchfulness, 'man's best friend' and faithful guardian.

Horse:

(The Chariot, Sun, Death, Knight Pentacles, Knight Swords, Knight Cups, Knight Wands, 6 Wands)

The horse can represent movement, action, energy, health and personal power

Lantern:

(The Hermit)

Lanterns are symbolic of enlightenment; lighting the way. Lamps can symbolise spiritual light, insight, awareness and perception.

Lightening:

(The Tower)

Lightning can symbolise divine intervention, immediate happenings and messages from the Universe.

Lightening can be symbolic of a flash of inspiration or creative energy that can help us find solutions to problems we are dealing with. Just as lightening comes before the thunder, lightning can also be a signal to warn us of an approaching storm. Divine intervention.

Lion:

(Strength, Wheel of Fortune, World, 2 Cups, Queen Wands, King Wands)

The need for courage. The Lion is the symbol of the astrological sign Leo which rules the heart. Leadership, strength and ability to achieve success.

Moon:

(High Priestess, Chariot, Moon, 2 Swords, Page Swords, 8 Cups)

The Moon is said to rule the subconscious, emotions and the senses. The Moon goes through a steady cycle each month as it waxes and wanes and disappears before being reborn again. Without the light of the Sun we would not be able to see the Moon. The quality of reflection belongs to the astrological Moon. The Moon can be symbolic of perception, receptivity, illumination, mystery, intuition, emotion, shadow and transition. The Moon can be symbolic of Karma and fate.

Mountains:

(Emperor , Lovers , Strength , Judgment , Fool , Page of Pentacles , Queen of Pentacles , 8 of Swords , 10 of Swords , 8 of Cups , Knight of Cups , Ace of Rods ,2 of Wands , 3 of Wands , 7 of Wands , Page of Wands , Knight of Wands)

Mountains can be symbolic of obstacles ahead. Climbing mountains or passing through them can indicate overcoming obstacles ... can a way be seen over or through the mountain? Mountains can suggest seclusion, isolation or goals that are hard to reach; experiences that will test your strength. Or a spiritual challenge. We may have to look beyond the mountain (beyond ourselves) to discover a sense of purpose, strength of character and transformation.

The Sea:

(2 of Pentacles , 5 of Swords , 6 of Swords , 10 of Swords , Page of Cups , Queen of Cups , King of Cups , 2 of Wands , 3 of Wands)

The sea is symbolic of emotions, dreams, dreams, the subconscious. The depth of the sea can indicate the depth of emotions. Are emotions ruling the head? How do circumstances suggest the emotional state?

Scales:

(Justice, 6 Pentacles)

Scales are symbolic of balance and judgement, harmony and fairness. Scales are the symbol of the astrological sign, Libra. Scales can represent karma.

Ship:

(Death, 2 Pentacles, King Cups, 3 Wands)

Ships in the tarot are symbolic of spiritual vehicles and progress. A ship can be symbolic of a journey in life, movement in life or the soul's journey.

Snake:

(Magician, Lovers, Wheel of Fortune 7 Cups)

Transition and transformation.

Waterfall:

(High Priestess, Empress, Queen of Swords)

Water can be symbolic of love, emotions, mystery and depth. Waterfalls are waters flowing, a steady flow of emotion or intuition.

Wheel:

(The Chariot, the Wheel of Fortune)

The Wheel in the tarot is symbolic of the wheel of life, change, the cycles of the cosmos

Numbers

Not only are there symbols in the images of the tarot cards but the number associated with each card, both in the Major and Minor arcana also has deeper meaning. The meanings of numbers given below are a general meaning. Different people might give a different interpretation of numbers and like everything in the tarot, you should go with what intuitively feels is right for you.

All numbers in the tarot (or any numerological study) can be balanced or unequal/unstable. When the balance is out of kilter something in our lives is causing disruption, a lack of equilibrium, uncertainty or disharmony.

Zero: Number of the future. First sign of something coming into being or about to take place. New potentials.

One: Beginnings, the first stages of a project, idea, relationship coming into being. One is the number of independence, leadership, courage, initiative and adventure. This number suggests a sense of direction, determination and originality. ... One is the start of every story.

Two: Duality and partnership. Choices. Empathy. Caring. Two is all about balance and peace-making, creating friendships, romance or partnerships. Qualities of two include: mediation, kindness, diplomacy, sensitivity, caution, intuition, cooperation.

Three: Resolution linked with thought and mental processes. Three is a creative number. Its qualities include: enthusiasm, celebration, inspiration, imagination, happiness, creativity, optimism, vision, animation and ease.

Four: After creation, ideas are turned into reality. Thought becomes form. Four is a practical number linked with solidity and stability. Determination, effort and discipline. Foundations. Qualities of this number include: application, dedication, management, concentration, efficiency.

Five: After building the foundations, number five gives the freedom to progress creative ideas and new enterprises. Five is the energy that encourages the promotion of new ideas and undertakings. Five relates to versatility and originality. Creativity promoting change. Qualities of five include: variety, adventure, movement, flexibility, conflict, change and invention.

Six: what purpose is there in life if there is no love, no-one to cherish, serve or care for? Six brings responsibility towards others and reminds us of the treasures in life. Six brings insight and knowing and the pursuit of wisdom. Qualities of six include: creativity, healing, passion, harmony, trust, serving, healing, domesticity and beauty.

Seven: After focusing on others it is time for 'self'. Seven is a number of contemplation and meditation. Deep thought activating awareness of spiritual dimension. This number represents the quest for wisdom and knowledge; wanting to make sense of it all. Qualities of seven include: research, analysis, intuition, reason, solitude, investigation, the unseen and understanding.

Eight: From inner awareness, it is time to come back down to earth. Eight is all about managing and supervising. It is a fundamental number which holds everything together with a sense of judgement. Qualities of eight include: authority, organisation, power, capability, skill, hard work, efficiency.

Nine: The power of love. With experience comes compassion, acceptance, forgiveness and benevolence. Nine holds the vibration of Universal love. Completion promoting truth and judgement. Qualities of nine include: intuition, emotion, imagination, creativity, love, benevolence, philanthropy, humanitarianism, dedication and devotion.

LEARNING TAROT SYSTEMATICALLY

So far you have learned that each suit has 10 numbered cards. There are four suits. Each suit relates to different areas of life.

Pentacles: Money and resources; possessions. Practical skills. Earth element. Zodiac signs: Taurus, Virgo and Capricorn

Swords: Thoughts and ideas. Communication. Movement. Air element. Zodiac signs: Gemini, Libra and Aquarius.

Cups: Emotions, relationships, spiritual growth. Water element. Zodiac signs: Cancer, Scorpio and Pisces.

Wands: energy, goals and ambitions. Work. Home/property/family life. Fire element. Zodiac signs: Aries, Sagittarius and Leo.

Each number has its own associations which can be linked to the suits. So to understand the 2 of pentacles for instance, look for the associations of the 2, link this with the associations of the Pentacles and you might get: "You might be putting a skill you have recently learned into practice."

Here is some brief associations of numbers and how these can be linked to the suits.

Aces

New beginnings or inspiration, sudden burst of energy for new starts. Inspiration. Taking the initiative. Situations just beginning. Potential of new situations. Seeds being sown. A gift or new opportunity.

Ace of Wands: Creativity. Confidence. Courage. Enthusiasm. Spark of inspiration. Passionate ideas. Imagination. Inspired to turn dreams into reality. Willing to put effort/action into achieving new goals.

Ace of Cups: Intuition. New romance. New friendships. Compassion. Consideration. Love. Bonding. Forgiveness. Empathy.

Ace of Pentacles: New financial offers. (promotion, new job opportunity, making money out of a hobby or new money making venture).

Ace of Swords: Clarity of mind. New ideas. New thoughts. Applying logic to overcome obstacles.

Twos

Raw energy starting to take shape to bring about what was begun by the Ace. Partnerships, working in unison. Balance. Dualism. Yin/yang. Light/dark. Two possibilities or two things in opposition. Choice between two possibilities. Sharing. A time of waiting/weighing up/making choices

Two of Wands: Two paths you can take to achieve same goal; two methods to **choose from,** two tools to use but you can only choose one. So there's a pause as you decide how to tackle a project from here. A time of planning. Decision leads to taking action.

Two of Cups: Shared feelings. Wanting to build on a friendship or new relationship. **The choice:** whether to put time into and share emotions with a new friend or partner. In existing relationship, choice to move it onto next level. Harmonious union of opposites. Compromise. Emotional balance.

Two of Pentacles: Balance here is juggling things in life: job, home, study. Trying to balance two important priorities and generally succeeding though it might take quite some effort. Multi-tasking. Just managing. **Choice between** different priorities.

Two of Swords: Choice between two opposing thoughts. Considering two sides of same argument. Analysing, deliberating, discussing, reconciling before making a decision. **Choice between** head and heart.

Threes

Starting to see things 'come together'; first stage complete. Creativity. Communication. Friendships. Activities shared. Loyalty. Bonding. (Visualise a triangle and the sides all meeting at the point at the top, bringing it all together to form the shape). So what is it that is 'coming together' in the suits of the tarot?

Three of Wands: **Coming together** of creative and entrepreneurial impulses already acted upon. Past planning and hard work is starting to get results. There will be opportunities to further develop skills.

Three of Cups: **Coming together** of a relationship or partnership making it feel more real, more secure. A celebration. A new level is reached. Strong feelings of friendship. Bonding. Time invested in friendships and relationships.

Three of Pentacles: **Coming together** of an arrangement or relationship that will be beneficial to all. Working with talented people as they combine talents and resources. Cooperative effort.

Three of Swords: Getting back together or **coming to** an end? A telling point for a relationship. A time of heartache, suffering and constant analysis. Sadness and sorrow. Letting go of a relationship/something in life that is causing unhappiness or finding a way to work through a painful experience. Focus is on separation and loss. Once over, this will bring feelings of relief. Will the point of the triangle bring things back together or pierce them, tearing them apart?

Fours

Establishment of security. Firm foundations have been established and can be built on. Structure. Stability.

Four of Wands: **Build on** 'structures' established so far. Security has been built through past hard work. Celebration of past hard work ... joyful moments shared with family, friends and workmates in celebration of a job well done.

Four of Cups: **Build on** emotional security already established. Build on trust, respect and loving bonds. Emotionally feeling a little bored and sorry for oneself but not seeing all the blessings life has to offer. Seeing the grass greener on the other side and not noticing the lush green grass beneath your feet. So lost in selfish thought (comparing one's life with another; moodiness and sulks) that there's a failure to appreciate their many blessings. After a spell of wishful thinking, go back and **build on** relationships/situations that have already been established.

 Four of Pentacles: Strong foundations have been laid leading to materialistic success. **Build on** this success without becoming too miserly. Knowing the value of money because of the hard work it has taken to reach this point. A time of stock-piling, collecting, of having achieved something tangible to build on. But be careful of being too possessive with money or material possessions.

Four of Swords: **Build on** your own inner resources (recoup your energy and build up your mental and emotional strength) to return to the challenges of life. Take time out. Take a break. A rest is needed from whatever chaos is going on around you. Rest and solitude is needed to help you u to help you recharge your batteries.

Fives

Uncertainty and/or change. Struggles. Competition or conflict. Loss. Challenge. Conflict leading to change.

Five of Wands: **Conflict between** equals. Conflict and inability to agree is blocking progress. Disagreements will go round in circles. Conflict is wasting energy and time.

Competitive atmosphere. Competition for work, a project, an opportunity .... Respect the opposition. There may be no 'right' solution or no happy agreement. May be a need to go with what feels right for you.

Five of Cups: **Conflicting emotions.** Is cup half full, half empty. Disappointments in a situation that didn't turn out as expected. Regret. Upset. Self-pity. Trouble letting go of past and moving on causing you to miss out on new opportunities. All is not lost.

Five of Pentacles: **Conflict between** needs and resources. Genuine poverty, loneliness and suffering; feeling left out in the cold. "Reach out" ... ask for help. You are not alone.

Five of Swords: **Conflict between** people, situations and/or conflict within. Conflict could indeed be plentiful. Disagreements lead to feelings of tension and hostility. Choose your battles. May win the argument but lose a friend. Any success will be bittersweet.

Six

Restoring balance after the disharmony of the fives. Creating harmony. Another stage complete (relating to the 3, final completion comes with the 9) Cooperation. Love. Consideration. Upliftment through success.

Six of Wands: **Upliftment through** a victorious achievement. All the hard work, past competition and effort was worth it bringing a sense of victory. Good fortune through past endeavours. Perfect balance. The victor is uplifted and others are happy to celebrate his success.

Six of Cups: **Upliftment through** nolstalgia. Looking back to see how far you've come. Focus on the positive. Be glad of the good things that have gone before and consider the way forward from there. Returning to past places, happy memories, reunions.

 Upliftment through being in touch with your inner-child and finding the child-like joy within.

Six of Pentacles: **Upliftment through** giving and/or receiving. Helping others financially or through time and effort. Charity work. Sharing. Paying it forward. Receiving financial help.

Six of Swords: **Upliftment through** moving away from a difficult situation. Leaving difficulties behind to move to a better place. This may lead to a change of jobs, duties or a change of residence. Healing has begun.

Sevens

Moving forward but in the right direction? Take time to reflect. Assess motives. Investigate. Meditate. Make choices. 7 is a mystical number: the number of the philosopher, sage, wisdom seeker. 7 reflects 'internal workings of the mind' so, what is going on 'within' rather than externally.

Seven of Wands: **Internal conflict** between 'own' beliefs, needs, intentions while knowing there is opposition from the outside. Digging in your heels and standing up for what you believe in. Fighting to protect all you have worked for so far. Continuing on 'own' path despite opposition. Courage to stand up for own beliefs.

Seven of Cups: **Internal conflict** between a number of wishes, choices and desires. Dreaming of what could be is all very well but without a 'choice' being made, nothing will come out of it.

Seven of Pentacles: **Internal conflict** between continuing with past (successful) efforts or trying different methods, paths, to move forward. A pause as you appreciate the outcome of all your past hard work (pentacles, work, effort, labour) and start to assess how best to spend your time in the future to bring similar success. Do you continue as you have been going or diversify, or try something new?

Seven of Swords: **Internal conflict** between right and wrong. What motivates actions? Someone engaging in devious activity (sitter or someone in their life) that leads to ethical considerations. Someone prying (again sitter or someone prying into their life). Need to respect other people's privacy and vice-versa.

Eights

8 is the number of infinity. Material possessions and money. Mental challenges to overcome (swords). Applying skills and past experience in useful ways (pentacles). Walking away from emotional situations which requires inner strength to find greater fulfilment (cups). Accomplishment through swift action (Wands) and coordinated effort. Eight relates to cycles (think of the flow of the circle at the top of the 8 into the bottom then up again): endings and new opportunities. Breaking free from restrictions.

Eight of Wands: Breaking free! **Breaking free** and moving forward with energy and enthusiasm. Exciting opportunities. Strike while the iron is hot. Quick developments. A lot happening in a short space of time.

Eight of Cups: **Breaking free** from an intensely emotional situation and accepting it is time to move on. A relationship/situation is no longer bringing the happiness, satisfaction or fulfilment it used to. There will always be sadness in breaking away but the disappointment in having put so much into a situation that is not going to change has left you emotionally exhausted. It can be fearful walking away from the past and into the unknown but it may be time to cut ties and break free.

Eight of Pentacles: **Breaking free** from a time of enjoying existing skills to find ways to make better use of your talents. This could lead to an apprenticeship, a course of study, a training course ... gaining new experiences in order to make better use of your skills. – New starts are likely in career, finances, education to 'perfect' existing talents,

knowledge and skills. Hard work will be necessary. Success won't be achieved overnight but dedication will get results.

Eight of Swords: **Breaking free** from feelings of being trapped, unable to move or feeling powerless BY taking back your own power. Making a painful decision. Take off the blindfold and what appears to be impossible, can be overcome.

Nines

9 brings completion and new awareness of 'self'. Wisdom through past experiences. Coming to terms with the person you are as a result of your past experiences.

Nine of Wands: **Coming to terms** with your inner strength and resourcefulness. The end is near and despite feeling completely drained and exhausted, it is not the time to give up. One final effort is all it will take to achieve your goal. You are capable of more than you realise.

Nine of Cups: **Coming to terms** with the idea that the success you craved will be fleeting. But do enjoy it while you can. On achieving your dreams, new ones will be formed. Enjoy the moment - there is a lot to be happy about – and be ready to move on to a brighter future.

Nine of Pentacles: **Coming to terms** with your own success which can add to your confidence. Projects/aims/work has been completed through effort and faith in your ability to be able to achieve. Enjoy the fruits of your labour. It is well deserved. A phase is complete. Prepare yourself for new beginnings ahead.

Nine of Swords: **Coming to terms** with fears and anxieties and recognising that worries are being magnified in your mind, adding to your despair. Negative emotions should not be allowed to prevent you from pursuing new opportunities.

Tens

The culmination of a chapter in life. Celebration in readiness for new beginnings (Ace). (1 plus 0 = 1 ... transition between the endings represented by 9 and new starts represented with Ace). Accepting (through analysis) that it is time to cut ties – this can be a painful time if seen in the swords. Letting go of old thought patterns or beliefs.

Ten of Wands: **Letting go** of responsibilities, commitments, situations that have become too burdensome.

Ten of Cups: **Letting go** of all emotions that have been holding you back: guilt, pride, perfectionism, negativity to discover the true source of happiness lies within. – A time when relationships are joyful, you feel good about your personal beliefs and values and family life is wonderful.

Ten of Pentacles: **Letting go** of doubts thanks to the successful conclusion of a hard working phase in life. There is success, accomplishment and final proof that you are capable of making great achievements. Focus is on family, financial security and tradition/heritage.

Ten of Swords: **Letting go** of past and present painful experiences that have brought sorrow, loss, disappointment, anger. Let go and accept circumstances as they now are. You have been as low as you can go and it is time to learn from these experiences, from the pain and darkness. You have been through many challenges. Trust a new day will soon dawn.

Other considerations:

From the Aces (cards of new beginnings), the 2s and 3s bring 'shared experiences'.

4s bring opportunities to 'build on' what has been established so far. Brings 'structure' into your life.

5s bring conflict leading to: 6 restoring balance.

7s to 9s focus on single characters (in Ryder Waite deck) or there are no characters in the images emphasising a time of going within, isolation or working on 'self' to move forward to bring us to:

10 ... endings in readiness for new beginnings.

Colours

What might the colours in the images on tarot cards represent? Here are just some suggestions, again you should go with what the colour intuitively means to you:

Blue: Blue represents intuition, feelings, the subconscious. This colour makes you think of the sea and the sky. It has depth. It is the colour associated with loyalty and truth. Blue can bring hope, clarity and cooperation.

Black: Black can represent power, sorrow, death and darkness. Grieving for something that is lost. A transition or tunnel we must move through in order to find the light.

Gold: Success and spiritual learning. Riches and wealth. Think of the Sun in all its splendour. Rewards and success.

Green: Abundance and fertility. Nature. Money. Wealth. Green is the colour of spring and new beginnings. Green is for healing, nurturing and soothing.

Orange: Happiness and good cheer. Energy and ambition. Action and sociability.

Red: Love, strength and passion. Anger and aggression.

Silver: Contemplation. Hidden wisdom. Mystery.

White: Purity, truth, peace and enlightenment.

Elements

The Suits in the tarot correspond to the elements: Fire, Earth, Air and Water. Everything in the material world can be linked to one or more of the elements. Associating the suits with their element helps us recognise the areas each suit represents.

Fire – Wands (also known as Staves, Batons or Rods) associated with energy, growth and development. Willpower and ambition.

Earth – Pentacles (also known as Disks or Coins) associated with money, business, material security, home life, growth, inheritance and riches. Earth is linked with steadiness and practicality; the mundane side of life: routine and responsibilities as well as fertility, conception, the seasons and the cycles of life.

Air – Swords associated with ideas, intellectual development, rational decisions, communication including technological communication, science and logic and the written word.

Water   Cups associated with feelings, relationships, intuition and creativity. Water and the Cups cards can represent our emotional and spiritual experiences. Happiness, joy, love and compassion as well as our psychic development.

Next Exercise:

Choose a tarot card with a character on and try to get into that character's head. Write a few notes from that person's perspective and what he or she is seeing around him (describe The landscape of the card through that person's eyes).

Choose a tarot card and write a story about the card, the characters in the card, what they are doing, feeling, planning. What lessons might they learn from what they are going through? (Feedback from our students on this exercise will be included at the end of this book).

Four
The Minor Arcana

The Difference between Major and Minor Arcana and understanding the Upright and Reversed Meanings of the Cards

Looking at the Minor Arcana

We have seen how the Major Arcana represented major themes in our lives and experiences. The 56 cards in the Minor Arcana represent everyday experiences we all go through at some time in our lives and relationships.

As a quick reminder, these 56 cards are divided into four suits: Wands, Cups, Pentacles and Swords. These suits are associated with different qualities. Wand cards are symbolic of creativity, action and movement. Cups cards represent emotion and spirituality, love and family. Swords are cards of thought, intellect and communication. Pentacles are the suit of material concerns, crafts, finances and practicality.

This lesson will give you interpretations of the minor arcana. Again, these are just suggestions and the more you work with your tarot cards, the more you will start to rely on your intuitive responses when giving readings.

The Cups Tarot Cards

Element: Water

Zodiac Signs: Cancer, Scorpio and Pisces

Season: Spring

If a reading contains many cups expect situations to contain a lot of emotion and powerful feelings.

Ace of Cups

Upright: New creative seeds being sown. A new relationship or friendship. Fertility, growth. A sense of joy and wellbeing. A time of pleasure and contentment.

Reversed: Anxiety over a relationship or creative potential. Feelings of sadness or loneliness.

Two of Cups

Upright: Focuses on relationships and friendship. The 'getting to know you' stage of a love affair. Partnerships developing. New relationships being formed. This is a relationship already begun but is starting to deepen. Bonding and commitments.

Reversed: Disharmony in relationships. Commitments falling apart, partnerships or friendships starting to falter. A time of arguments, conflict, disagreements and broken promises.

Three of Cups

Upright: Time of celebration. If there have been problems these have been overcome. Sense of fulfilment. Promises being made. Abundance. Blessings. Pregnancy.

Reversed: Too much of a good thing isn't always good for you. Possible over-indulgence in pleasurable past-times, food or alcohol. Recklessness. Thoughtlessness towards others. What could have been great is being ruined by someone's selfish behaviour.

Four of Cups

Upright: A time of assessment and meditation. Focusing on emotions. So wrapped up in own feelings could miss out on good opportunities. Not noticing what's going on around and about because there's such an intense focus on self and feelings.

Reversed: Be open to new opportunities, new relationships or friendships, new offers. Push worries aside as positive change is likely. Rather than dwell on negatives, turn all this energy around and direct it on positive opportunities that help you move forward.

Five of Cups

Upright: Emotional loss and feelings of having been betrayed. Feeling a little miserable and lonely. There may be frustration or regret and concentrating on all that has been lost but overlooking the opportunities that still remain. All is not lost as this is also a card of hope. The message is: don't give in to regret and depression. Count your blessings.

Reversed: Instead of thinking about all that is going wrong, consider what has gone right for you. A situation may be difficult but all is not lost. There is still a chance to put it right or to make amends. Someone might return after leaving.

Six of Cups

Upright: Happy memories. Reminiscing alone or with old friends. Meeting up with people from the past and enjoying happy reunions. Changes are in the early stages. They are not hugely apparent but they will bring contentment. Possible new employment.

Reversed: Reluctance to face up to possible changes that are happening. Tendency to live in the past and having a hard time facing the future. Feels a lack of emotional strength.

Seven of Cups

Upright: Getting in touch with emotions. Reflection. A time of spiritual development and delving inwards before making decisions. Are senses being clouded by emotion. Be cautious and be wise about the choices that are ahead.

Reversed: Confusion and uncertainty. Focus on emotions and desires in order to understand what you are going through. It's important to remember that material success is not everything and this could well lead to spiritual poverty. Persist in your intentions and confusion will be replaced with spiritual strength.

Eight of Cups

Upright: A need for emotional and spiritual contemplation. It is time to walk away from a stressful situation. A radical change is necessary and this means either a current situation or relationship has to change or it is time to walk away from it. Breaking away from the past will take you on to a new and more significant path.

Reversed: There is confusion about which direction to head in. There is unhappiness and dissatisfaction but some uncertainty about which way to go. Has a situation or relationship passed its sell-by date yet you continue to hang on, knowing that it is already over?

Nine of Cups

Upright: Happiness and harmony. Family celebration. Also called the Wish Card. Past worries and anxieties will vanish. Success, good health and good fortune.

Reversed: Don't give up hope. Things are looking up. Difficulties will soon be over. Both reversed and upright this is a lovely card to turn up in a reading.

Ten of Cups

Upright: Fulfilment of hopes and dreams. A chapter is coming to a close, a long-term goal is reached. Life and relationships are good. Lots of happiness and yet a little niggle ... something in the back of your mind tells you that something new is on its way.

Reversed: Happiness is all around you now so don't miss out. Live in the moment. Are you so focused on the future that you aren't taking full advantage of the blessings around you now?

Page of Cups

Upright: A pleasing message will be received. The start of a new romance or friendship. A marriage or birth. Links with a sensitive and gentle person. There will be good news associated with this person.

Reversed: Information in an email or text message is not to be trusted. Beware of malicious gossip and rumours. News received may not be what was expected.

Knight of Cups

Upright: Stick to the tried and tested route. Follow the most direct path ahead. Avoid experimentation or you will be easily distracted. A social invitation is possible or the start of a creative project. Time to turn ideas into reality. Balance ideas with action or nothing will come out of them.

Reversed: Stay in control of your emotions. Don't act without thinking.

Queen of Cups

Upright: Trust your intuition. There is a pleasant mix of sensitivity, caution and understanding. A good time to meditate and do some soul searching.

Reversed: Avoid making promises you can't keep. You may mean well but could be taking on more than you can chew. Someone who tends to exaggerate the truth could be causing problems in relationships.

King of Cups

Upright: A man of authority and success will offer some wise advice. This person has a caring nature and his advice can be relied on.

Reversed: Be careful who you trust. Even professionals have been known to get it wrong. Someone who looks as if he knows what he's talking about probably hasn't got a clue.

The Wands Tarot Cards

Element: Fire

Zodiac Signs: Aries, Leo and Sagittarius

Season: Summer

If a reading contains many Wands, expect life to be busy with plenty to do either at home, at work or with regard to hobby and outdoor interests. May be searching for a purpose.

Ace of Wands

Upright: A burst of energy can bring about new creative or business beginnings. Positive attitude brings positive results.

Reversed: Inactive. No enthusiasm or not willing to put in the effort necessary to achieve.

Two of Wands

Upright: Opportunity to progress in career. May involve some form of partnership. Laying the foundations of a new venture. New undertakings have tremendous potential for success.

Reversed: Opportunities missed through pessimism or uncertainty.

Three of Wands

Upright: While most projects are going well, this is a good time to continue as planned but also to put out feelers for possible new ventures.

Reversed: Possible delays and setbacks. Projects aren't turning out as anticipated.

Four of Wands

Upright: Projects are brought to a successful conclusion. A goal is achieved. Celebration in the air.

Reversed: An opportunity may have strings attached. Disorganisation can cause problems.

Five of Wands

Upright: An element of competition is in the air but this can be good and bring out the best in you.

Reversed: a competitive atmosphere serves no useful purpose and blocks progress.

Six of Wands

Upright: Achievement, success and victory. Confidence is high. You have plenty reason to feel proud of your current achievements.

Reversed: A goal may not be reached, a test failed, a wish is not granted. Can always try again.

Seven of Wands

Upright: Conflict and confrontation. It's no use hiding. Best to face challenges head on. There are competitors who will try to undermine you. Stand up for what you believe in.

Reversed: A lack of confidence or tendency to avoid conflict and challenge can lead to giving in on a current aim.

Eight of Wands

Upright: A sudden burst of purposeful energy leading to prompt action taken. Action will be swift. Progress is likely towards goals.

Reversed: Delay in progress to achieving aims. Possible travel disruptions.

Nine of Wands

Upright: You may have set yourself some difficult goals. It might feel as if you're running out of energy and resources and you wonder whether you will reach your aim. Keep on trying as there is energy in reserve you can tap into when you need it.

Reversed: Obstacles are likely to get in the way of the achievement of a current aim.

Ten of Wands

Upright: You have been through a lot. You have achieved a lot. Now is the time to re-assess your goals and work out where you might go from here. A new cycle probably relating to your career is about to begin.

Reversed: Have you taken on more than you can chew? It may be necessary to reconsider your commitments with a view to reducing responsibilities.

Page of Wands

Upright: Energy mixes with ideas and can bring about tangible results. Enthusiasm for new projects is infectious.

Reversed: A creative block could prevent you from moving forward. Lack of direction.

Knight of Wands

Upright: Movement is on the cards. A journey of self-discovery.

Reversed: Appearances can be deceptive. A con artist will try to deceive. Don't let impatience get the better of you.

Queen of Wands

Upright: A jealous woman could be stirring up trouble. Avoid situations of conflict if possible.

Upright: A time to take positive action. Leadership qualities are on show. Actions and decisions will bring material rewards.

Reversed: Delays could prevent you from reaching a current aim. Work your way through them one at a time. Avoid being too forceful in relationships.

King of Wands

Upright: Passion and energy can lead to great achievements. Countryside settings appeal now.

Reversed: Beware of spreading energy too thinly.

The Swords Tarot Cards

Element: Air

Zodiac Signs: Gemini, Libra and Aquarius

Season: Winter (sometimes spring)

If a reading contains many suggest that many aspects of life will need careful thought and analysis. A lot of emphasis on communication, possible arguments, disagreements and the need to find solutions to conflict.

Ace of Swords

Upright: Expect a powerful surge of mental energy which helps provide the drive and inspiration to start new ventures. Thoughts are clear. There may be a sense of Karma linked with current events.

Reversed: Sudden changes may not seem to work to your advantage. Arguments could lead to delayed or cancelled plans.

Two of Swords

Upright: Reveal your thoughts and feelings or misunderstandings could arise. There may be a sense of fumbling in the dark. Not certain of where certain aspects of your life are heading.

Reversed: Changes may be blessings in disguises.

Three of Swords

Upright: Confusion, upsets in relationships. Arguments could lead to a parting of the ways.

Reversed: Communications are breaking down. Misunderstandings. A relationship is coming to an end or has just ended.

Four of Swords

Upright: A time of rest and recuperation after an illness or the need to recharge mental or physical energies. Important to take a break and if this means turning off your mobile, spending less time on your computer and getting in touch with nature, so be it.

Reversed: A failure to rest and recoup your energy can lead to stress-related illnesses.

Five of Swords

Upright: Beware the gossips. There may be a feeling of not being good enough or of letting someone down. People can be manipulative.

Reversed: Sometimes it is better to cut your losses and run. Why continue fighting a losing battle? It doesn't mean you are weak to walk away.

Six of Swords

Upright: You're starting to move away from recent difficulties. The worst is behind you. You are moving forward now to a happier place.

Reversed: A temporary solution will be offered in a tense situation. This will give you a chance to take a rest before you decide what to do next.

Seven of Swords

Upright: Ideas flood your mind and although you might want to act on them all, it will be important to prioritise. You can't possibly do everything. Take care about whom you share information with or someone will try to steal your thunder.

Reversed: Be honest in all your dealings. If you tell untruths you could end up tripping over your own lies. Conversely, be careful who you trust.

Eight of Swords

Upright: It might feel as if you are stuck in a rut. Thinking outside the box may help you break out and into new areas. Heavy responsibilities will make it feel as if you are restricted but don't give up now. There are options available but you need to be in the right frame of mind to see these.

Reversed: A difficult phase is coming to an end. You are starting to see new options and feel ready to break away from a past limiting situation.

Nine of Swords

Upright: Worries keep you awake at night. Responsibility may be getting you down. Everything is getting on top of you. Fear, anxiety worry can be mentally and emotionally draining. Face up to difficult issues and you can break out of this dark phase of your life.

Reversed: You are starting to see the light at the end of the tunnel. Take heart: worries will soon ease.

Ten of Swords

Upright: Difficulties can lead to emotional upset, pain or endings. As hard as it is at the time, keep reminding yourself that as one door closes another will open. When you reach the bottom, there's only one way you can go and that's upwards.

Reversed: It's time to sweep all those negative thoughts out of your mind. Look for the positives and be open to new opportunities.

Page of Swords

Upright: An insightful young man. Interesting and creative communications.

Reversed: Check your motives before acting. Is someone being petty? Anxiety about the future.

Knight of Swords

Upright: Charming and intelligent young man who tends to be a risk-taker. Weigh up options. Guard against over-optimism.

Reversed: Someone is not adverse to treading on everyone else's toes in their desire to get ahead.

Queen of Swords

Upright: Independent and intelligent woman who can be secretive and mysterious.

Reversed: Someone who is allowing logic to rule making her cold and distant.

King of Swords

Upright: Courageous and intelligent man who will make sensible judgements. Good time to analyse situations and be ready to take the initiative.

Reversed: Someone who can be sarcastic and critical of everyone they meet.

The Pentacles Tarot Cards

Element: Earth

Zodiac Signs: Taurus, Virgo and Capricorn

Season: Autumn

If a reading contains many Pentacle cards this highlights practical concerns such as financial and material matters, property, skills necessary for life i.e. cooking, cleaning, crafts but also artistic and creative work. Also career matters and earning ability.

Ace of Pentacles

Upright: A prosperous phase begins. Possibility of receiving an unexpected sum of money.

Reversed: Money problems can cause uncertainty and anxiety.

Two of Pentacles

Upright: Good time to develop new skills that can be useful in your career. Possibility of making money out of a hobby.

Reversed: Demands for money can seem to come in faster than the money does. A sense of direction is needed is you expect to achieve.

Three of Pentacles

Upright: A career or financial goal is reached. An examination or test is passed, an interview is successful. This marks the start of a new and more lucrative phase.

Reversed: Delays and disturbances can block current goals.

Four of Pentacles

Upright: A more stable period financially. May be looking into buying some property.

Reversed: Financial worries; feeling strapped for cash.

Five of Pentacles

Upright: Financial difficulties. A testing time. Struggling to afford the necessities of life.

Reversed: A challenging situation. Look into the possibility of gaining funding or grants.

Six of Pentacles

Upright: A gift or money is received. Generosity abounds. Volunteer efforts bring emotional rewards.

Reversed: Caution is necessary in finances. Keep an eye on money and possessions to avoid loss.

Seven of Pentacles

Upright: Expect to work hard to get results. It might feel as if you aren't getting paid enough for all the work that you do.

Reversed: Exhausted physically and emotionally due to hard work and heavy responsibilities.

Eight of Pentacles

Upright: Development of new skills. May be reaching the end of a university or training course or signing up for one. Ability to apply knowledge and abilities in a practical and profitable way.

Reversed: May feel disgruntled in your job. Heavy responsibilities that aren't enjoyed. Is it time to start looking for a new job.

Nine of Pentacles

Upright: Past hard work brings its just rewards. Life is comfortable and pleasurable even. A little extra cash to pamper yourself and splash out on luxuries.

Reversed: Need to take care with money. Extravagant impulses could later be regretted.

Ten of Pentacles

Upright: Financial success. Life is pleasurable. Receipt of a bonus or inheritance or a loan offer.

Reversed: family or housemates aren't doing their share. Difficulties involving financial transactions.

Page of Pentacles

Upright: A young man with a careful and practical nature. You will be taking a sensible and calm approach to current problems.

Reversed: Easily distracted. There's a need to focus energy to get results.

Knight of Pentacles

Upright: A determined and methodical young man who will succeed through perseverance. Other people will find you honest and reliable. If you make a promise you will keep it.

Reversed: Anxiety about your future success can hold you back. Carelessness can lead to mistakes. Take it one step at a time and have more faith in yourself.

Queen of Pentacles

Upright: A reliable woman who will give sensible advice. Weigh up pros and cons before making a move. Practicality will get results.

Reversed: Work and other responsibilities might seem to take over your life. There may be worries about keeping on top of everyday bills.

King of Pentacles

Upright: A fatherly figure or good businessman who can offer career guidance or financial support. A successful business or creative venture. Make good use of your skills.

Reversed: A person who is materialistic and greedy or a workaholic. You might feel as if work is taking over your life. You could be questioning your social, work or partnership ties. Is someone all they really make themselves out to be?

Revision:

Remember that it can help to think of the number on the card and the general indication of that number then merge this with the quality of the suit i.e. all Aces relate to new beginnings and fresh opportunities. With the Ace of Wands, the Wands can be related to creativity, work, energy. So, the Ace of Wands can mark the start of a new adventure, birth or new beginning or fertility.

Revision of the meaning of numbers:

Here are some quick keywords to remind you of what numbers in the tarot (and other aspects of divination) can mean.

1 – Fresh start. New beginnings. New opportunities. Positive surge of energy.

2 – Partnerships, duality, balance of opposites. Conflict. Negotiation.

3 – Resolution of conflict (associated with the 2). Themes of threes i.e. Spirit, soul and matter, Father, mother and child.

4 – Structure (think of 4 walls of a house), stability and balance. Foundation. Boundaries.

5 – Change. Instability. Conflict. Possible loss, sorrow or misfortune.

6 – Harmony and communication.

7 – Experimentation. Risk (both positive and negative). Courage.

8 – Action. Movement. Taking steps to resolve a situation.

9 – Completion. Achievement. Celebration.

10 – Completion. Lessons Learned. Endings in readiness for new beginnings. Spiritual growth.

****

Minor Arcana Exercise

Choose four cards from the minor arcana of the same number
i.e. the four of cups, four of wands, four of swords and four of
pentacles. Now compare the similarities and differences in
these cards. (Feedback to this exercise from our students will
be included at the end of this book).

Five
Reading the Tarot for Yourself and Others

Quick Revision of what has been learned so far. Understanding the reason to ground, cleanse and protect when giving readings. Understanding use of tarot spreads and how to give a reading.

You are almost ready to read cards for yourself and others, but before we do this, here's a quick summary of what you have already learned so far.

The Major Arcana

There are 22 Major Arcana cards numbered from 0 (the Fool) to 21 (the World). These cards are 'major' in that they reflect major events in life and their strength of imagery reflect this.

Minor Arcana

When beginning tarot readings, the Minor Arcana might seem daunting to get your head around as new readers get bogged down trying to learn the endless meanings of the cards. This is not what is important. General readings are useful in helping you understand your cards and learning tarot as with any form of spiritual development is an on-going process. You might enjoy looking up cards on the internet and studying what they mean to other people. If any of this resonates with you, you might take some of it and use it in your own readings. What's most important is how you work with your cards, the impressions you feel and the insights you perceive – your intuitive response.

Reversed Cards

You can choose to use reversed cards to give a reading more depth. Again don't worry too much about reversed card meanings. If you understand the upright meaning of the card, the energy that is blocked as shown by a reversed card will come to you.

Elements

The four suits can be related to the four vital elements: Fire, Earth, Air and Water.

Fire = Wands: creative matters and enterprising, expansive aspects of life

Earth = Pentacles/Coins: material matters and all things of a fixed and solid nature

Air = Swords: ideas, intelligence, communication and logic

Water = Cups: Love. Emotional and spiritual matters.

Numbers and Colours

Numbers of each card and the colours used in the images are also important. Briefly, 1 can represent new starts, seeds being sown, a gift. 2: balance and harmony; choice 3: regeneration and creativity; abundance. 4: stability, structure and solidity. 5: instability, change and challenges. 6: reinforcement, consolidation, giving and support. 7: reflection, speculation, looking ahead, intuition. 8: attainment, material energy, mastering, movement. 9: experience, results, understanding, fulfilment of the suit. 10: finality, completeness, culmination, transition.

The Tarot Card Reading

You are now ready to begin on reading the tarot, either for yourself or for others. Remember that it will take time for your confidence to build.

It won't happen overnight. Even if you feel you have a good grasp of the basic meanings of all the cards and have been able to intuitively tune into the images so far, it can feel a little overwhelming to suddenly be faced with reading a number of cards grouped together in a spread.

Once you relax into the reading, you may be surprised by how the interpretation will flow and how you can see how one card might support another or add a little extra information to what you have already seen in another card in the spread.

Ground, Cleanse and Protect

Before doing any kind of psychic work it is good to have knowledge of basic psychic defence. Everyone and everything around you gives off energy. You might notice you often feel uplifted in the company of a certain friend whereas other people leave you feel drained and exhausted every time you see them or are in contact with them. The energy you soak in from the environment around you can affect you. If you are constantly being subjected to another person's negative energy, this can have an impact on your emotions and your spiritual and physical health. Your energy interacts all the time with outside energies. When reading the tarot, it is important to learn how to ground, centre, cleanse and protect yourself from allowing other people's energy to enter your aura. This exercise should be carried out between each reading and even as a daily routine, as you go to bed at night. It can also help you to regain your spiritual, emotional and physical equilibrium.

Grounding

There are many ways you can ground yourself (connecting with the earth and drawing energy from the earth or Mother Nature). One of the most common techniques is for you to imagine you are a tree. Breathe in slowly and deeply through your nose and out through your mouth. Now try to imagine roots going down deep into the earth from the soles of your feet, extending deeper into the earth beneath you. If it helps you can imagine your roots wrapping around a huge crystal, stone or boulder as they keep you tied to the earth. This is called grounding and can be used whenever you feel spaced-out.

Cleanse

Imagine an orb of pure white light hovering above your head. See it gaining in strength, growing brighter and stronger with every breath you take. Now visualise this ball of bright white light flowing down like a waterfall over your head and through your aura, flowing over your shoulders and down to the ground, cleansing your energy field.

Next imagine this pure white light flowing down into your body through your crown chakra and cascading through your other chakras: the throat, the heart, the solar plexus, the sacral chakra and root chakra and then down through your legs and out through the soles of your feet. Visualise this pure white light cleansing all your chakras, pushing all negative energy downwards until it seeps away into the earth beneath your feet. Your energy field has been cleansed.

Shield

Shielding is a technique used to block out harmful energies while still letting harmless and loving energies in. Imagine a bubble of white or blue light surrounding your body, protecting you. Visualise yourself as being completely surrounded by this bubble of light. This is your protective bubble. Another shielding method is to surround yourself by a circle of mirrors with their reflective side facing away from you and this will allow positive, loving energies in and reflect negative energies away. Always ask that the negative energies be returned to where they came from with love.

Reading the Tarot

Before starting your reading you might decide whether you are going to read reversed cards as a separate meaning to upright ones or not.

Some readers will read a card in the same way whether it is reversed or upright and that's okay if you would prefer to do this too. If you choose to read reversals differently, be consistent. Remember too that not all reversed cards mean the opposite of the upright card. Think of reversed cards in terms of strength and energy. When a card is upright, it is strong and its energy is flowing positively. When a card is reversed, its position is weaker. Its energy may be blocked, thwarted, increasing or decreasing. – Trust your intuition to guide you on its meaning.

Shuffling the Cards

Before you start you reading you might like to shuffle the cards first or you may prefer to hand them straight to your sitter for them to shuffle. Some readers shuffle for the sitter (and this can be done if you are reading for someone on-line) however if the sitter is in the room with me, I prefer that they shuffle themselves so the cards can pick up on their energy.

There is no right or wrong way to shuffle the cards. Some larger tarot cards can be harder to handle. Shuffle and move the cards around until you feel ready to stop. Once the cards are shuffled, ask the sitter to cut the cards into three piles then the cards back on top of each other before handing them to you.

Decide on your spread. Once you decide on this, keep the cards in the order of the desired spread i.e. for a three card, past, present and future reading, card one will represent the past, card two, the present and card three the future.

Which Spread?

There are a number of spreads you might choose from when doing a reading and I'd recommend that you experiment with a few until you find a one that works best for you. The spreads or layout is how the cards are dealt out in order to do a reading. The layout can add to your reading because this will give you the frame or context in which to interpret and relate the cards. These can vary from a one-card reading where there are no cards to compare and contrast, three card reading and upwards. You may, at first, choose to start with basic three card readings. Each card, one, two and three will represent an area or phase of life for instance:

Past, Present and Future.

Current happenings, Coming happenings, Conclusion

Mind, Body and Spirit

Possibilities, Challenges, Advantages

Variations on Five Card spreads include:

1 Your potential

2 Gifts you are aware of

3 What is blocking you from using your gifts

4 Gifts you aren't aware of

5 What will help you share your gifts

1 What you known

2 What you aren't aware of

3 What others know

4 What others aren't aware of

5 Outcome

1 Present situation

2 Possible obstacles

3 Positive influences

4 Near future

5 Long term consequences

1 Distant Past

2 Recent Past

3 Present

4 Near future

5 Distant Future

5 card relationship spread:

1 Strengths in the Relationship

2 Weaknesses in the relationship

3 Benefits of the relationship

4 Happiness within the relationship

5 Future of the relationship

There are as many Tarot spreads as there are tarot readers. Some are a lot more complicated than others and will require a good working knowledge of the cards before they can be tackled but it is entirely possible to get good results with simple layouts as suggested above.

How to Read your Cards

You now have your cards laid out in a spread in front of you and you are ready to read the cards. As well as bearing in mind the position of each card and what they relate to, other things to bear in mind when reading the cards are:

Is there a predominance of one element?

Is an element missing?

How many major arcana in the spread – the more major arcana the more it is likely that the querent is going through a major phase in life

Look at the numbers of the cards and think about what these might be saying to you

What are the major symbols in the cards that stand out to you?

Are you seeing a predominance of a colour or suit?

Remember that (if you have chosen to read reversed cards), reversed cards can signify that the positive outcome of the upright card is frustrated, blocked or avoided. Reversed cards aren't necessarily negative and can show signs of hope when the upright meaning is a tense one.

Don't worry if your mind goes blank when you are at first presented with the cards. Take your time to 'get into' your reading. Take it slowly and you will be surprised to find yourself slowly linking the cards together.

You might read one card, move on to another and then return to a previous card as you can see how they link together and work with each other to form an overall picture.

Notice how you intuitively react to each card. Remember that the book-meanings of the cards aren't as important as YOUR intuitive reactions. Your feelings come from the images as they speak to you. The more you read the tarot, the quicker you will link with your cards.

Ending the Reading

Once the reading is over, you might write a summary in your Tarot journal as this is useful to return to in the future.

Shuffle the cards to clear them of energy from this reading.

Tarot Exercises for your Journal

(i) Shuffle all your cards and put them on the table in front of you face down.

Now take the card at the top of the pile, face up.

Study this card and think about an event, situation or theme in your life, present or past that you might associate with this card.

Meditate on this situation for a while. How did it begin? How did it unfold? How did it conclude? Was it ever resolved?

Add your thoughts to your journal.. You might do this with other cards too as this will help you place your own meanings to the cards.

Exercise (ii)

Sort your tarot cards into three piles: court cards, numbered cards from each suit (four piles) and the Major Arcana.

Shuffle each of the piles individually.

Take the top card from the court cards pile. Imagine a scenario for this character. It might be a workplace, relationship, holiday scenario or life event. Give your mind free rein to wander.

Take one of the numbered cards from each of the four piles.

Arrange these cards in a cross (North, South, East and West, with the court card in the middle).

Draw the top card from the Major Arcana Pile. Put this face down beside the others. This will be the outcome.

Now interpret the Minor Arcana cards in relation to the scenario you imagined for the character and the outcome as shown by the Major Arcana card.

Exercise (iii)

Experiment with Card Combinations:

When you are reading a spread, you aren't just looking at each individual card, you will be reading the cards together, as they relate to and interact with each other. Studying card combinations will help you to do this more easily. Shuffle your cards and deal out two, placing them next to each other. Now consider the images in the cards. Think of the people, events, location, circumstances in the cards and how these combine. This helps give you a deeper understanding of the cards and greater confidence when reading tarot card spreads. Do this a number of times.

Six
Enjoying your Tarot Cards

How to enjoy using your Tarot Cards and understanding how the tarot can be used as a tool for self-growth, spiritual development and enhancing your creativity.

The Tarot and You

Using your cards to do readings for yourself, your family and friends is only one of several ways you can enjoy your cards. The Tarot can be a wonderful tool for self-growth, spiritual development and understanding and to enhance your creativity.

The Tarot and Meditation

The tarot can be an effective and exciting tool for meditation; here's how tarot cards might enhance your understanding of yourself and your spirituality.

Many people think of the tarot only in connection with fortune telling, gypsies and the occult but in fact tarot cards have a number of useful purposes including offering greater insight into your subconscious, how you feel about yourself and how you might develop your spirituality. As a tool for meditation, the rich and colourful symbolism in tarot cards can be a great way to enhance life and a person's awareness of themselves. Meditating with tarot cards can also be an emotionally healing and spiritually uplifting experience.

Every card has its own meaning and often what one card means for one person is different for another. For that reason you can discover for yourself, through meditating on each card, what it means to you and how each tarot card might help develop your spirituality and enhance your understanding of yourself, your life and relationships.

Just as a tarot card reading might give you answers to some questions on your mind, meditating on a tarot card or on a number of tarot cards can reveal choices or options you may not have previously considered.

If you have never meditated before, don't worry that you will make mistakes or won't reach the deep levels others who are more experienced might talk about when they describe their meditations. It might seem as if some use meditation to go into a trance but you don't necessarily have to reach a trance-like state to meditate: just look on meditation as a way to help you relax and to expand your consciousness.

Using a tarot card for meditating can be a great way to start your journey inward. All you have to do is find a quiet place where you won't be disturbed. Settle yourself in a comfortable position and choose the tarot card on which you would like to meditate. Settle your eyes on the card and allow a pleasant, dream-like state to come over you. Feel the card draw your mind into its image and don't try to control your thoughts; let them go wherever they take you. You might get further impressions of the card in your mind or your thoughts might wander to places you don't normally go.

It's always a good idea to note down anything you see or experience immediately after the meditation before it fades. This will be a good reference too, to refer to later when you might wish to compare your meditation experiences with each card so as to learn what each tarot card might mean for you.

To give you an idea on how you might begin these exercises if all this sounds very strange to you, the following gives a brief suggestion on which of the cards in the major arcana you might choose for your meditation depending on the question currently on your mind or current circumstances:

The Fool

Is it time to move on? The Fool is a good card to use for meditation when thinking about the future.

The Magician

Focus on the Magician when a question needs deep analysis.

The High Priestess

How might you remember your dreams? The High Priestess will always link you with your intuition and spiritual side when this tarot card is used for meditation.

The Empress

Is it time to get started on home improvement projects? The Empress is a good card to focus on if you're thinking about having a baby or other family matters.

The Emperor

Will you get the official support you need for your ideas? Meditate on the Emperor when you need advice or guidance from someone you can trust.

The Hierophant

Confused about religion? If so the Hierophant will help you become more aware of your spirituality and intuitive side.

The Lovers

Use the Lovers tarot card for meditation when torn between two choices or when trying to resolve difficulties in romance.

The Chariot

Travel matters and communication issues of all sorts can be more easily understood by meditating on the Chariot tarot card.

Strength

When life is challenging and heavy demands are being made of you, meditate on Strength tarot card to find ways to ensure you don't over stress yourself.

The Hermit

The Hermit is a peaceful card for meditation and its symbolism will take you to quiet, serene places where you feel at ease with yourself.

The Wheel of Fortune

If it seems as if things are changing and you have no control over your life the Wheel of Fortune is the card to focus on now.

Justice

Justice can play a key role in helping your subconscious tune into the right and wrong things that are going on in your life at a specific moment.

The Hanged Man

If it feels as if you are giving too much of yourself to others and aren't getting enough time for yourself, the Hanged Man will help you find more balance in life.

Death

When relationships, commitments and chapters in your life are coming to an end and you sense a new beginning is imminent, Death is a good card to choose for your meditation exercise.

Temperance

Peace and harmony can be found when using Temperance for meditation. This tarot card will take you to tranquil places where you can relax and free yourself of the stress of everyday living.

The Devil

The Devil tarot card is the one to choose if you're feeling negative, resentful or aggrieved in any way.

The Tower

Meditate on the Tower when trying to make sense of changes in your life that may have occurred unexpectedly.

The Star

If needing fresh hope or a sprinkling of optimism in your life, focus on the Star and enjoy the happy thoughts this might bring.

The Moon

This card will help you tune into your intuition and deal with confusion linked with psychic experiences.

The Sun

The Sun is a beautiful tarot card to meditate on when hoping for success, looking for love or searching for spiritual support.

Judgement

Judgement, when used for meditation, might help you understand reasons behind recent experiences and how to make decisions that won't lead to future regrets.

The World

Travel questions might be answered through meditating on the World tarot card.

Tarot and Creativity

If you enjoy writing you could use your tarot cards to write a story or to help you overcome writer's block. Choose two or three cards and then use the images to create a short story.

You might draw a card to represent the protagonist, another card to represent a character he or she will meet during the plot (which will be shown by the next card drawn.)

Using your cards as a tool for creative development can help you build a more intimate relationship with your cards.

Write a poem a day based on a tarot card.

If you are feeling artistic, you might sketch or paint images that come to your mind when you think of a particular card.

Tarot Exercise – Who, What, When, Where and Why?

Shuffle the cards and choose one. Study this card and answer the following questions.

Who? ... Who does this card remind you of? i.e. The Empress could be someone who offers you emotional fulfilment. Or which side of yourself does this card remind you of. The Empress might be your creative and nurturing side. If this card draws attention to your current goals, a hope or wish, who do you need on your side to help you bring them about?

What? What are the issues that might be facing you according to this card? Have you addressed these lately and are you aware of your priorities. Are you clear about what these issues may mean and how they might affect your life in the future? Can you work on them to understand them as fully as possible? ... so in the case of the Empress, this could relate to an emotional situation which could involve planting new creative seeds, a birth, the start of something new in your family life. There may be no issues as such if this card points to an emotionally satisfying episode but it is always good to be aware of the possibilities that might come out of this situation.

Why? Why should this situation matter to you? Should it make you happy, contented, hopeful? Should it worry you? Is there something you are hoping to achieve for instance with the Empress are you hoping to develop your creativity or your spiritual side? Is this a purpose you truly believe in and you should make a priority?

When? When should you start focusing on the issues brought up by this card? Could now be the right time? Should you wait for a while until you feel more prepared?

Sometimes the card will give the answer for instance the Four of Swords will suggest that this is a time to pause and recoup your energies before making your next move.

Finally, in conclusion, ask:

How? ... How might you bring about the intentions implied by this card? Which skills might you draw on or develop in order to reach these goals? How can you put what you are learning now into practice?

TAROT EXERCISE – SELF-READING

To do this fun reading, first of all you need to know the card that relates to you and you can do this from your Sun Sign. Look at the list below and make a note of the card that relates to your sign.

Aries = Emperor

Taurus = Hierophant

Gemini = Lovers

Cancer = Chariot

Leo = Strength

Virgo = Hermit

Libra = Justice

Scorpio = Death

Sagittarius = Temperance

Capricorn = Devil

Aquarius = Star

Pisces = Moon

Now shuffle your cards. Then start dealing them out one after another until you come to the card that relates to you. Once you find this, make a note of the cards on either side of this. The card before it will relate to your past (a situation that is still affecting you now) and the card after it relates to your PRESENT and general scenario as relating to that situation. Now interpret those cards.

Seven
Students' Feedback to Exercises

Feedback from Students to Exercises in this Book.

As promised previously, here is some of the feedback we have received by our students to the exercises shared in previous chapters of this book. You might find this helpful when carrying out the exercises and it is fun, too, to compare.

Exercise 1, Chapter 1

How well are you doing with this exercise?– Remember that what's most important is what your cards mean to you: your intuitive responses. This means that there is no right or wrong way of reading the tarot. Providing you are serious about doing readings and your aim is to offer the highest quality reading you can give, you are on the right track.

This book also includes the traditional meanings of the cards but what comes to you from your cards will always be right for you. – Keep these notes on each card. Add them to your tarot journal. Date them and then you might return to them later to compare how you feel about your cards further down the line to how you did at the start of this wonderful learning journey. You might find that the more you work with your cards, your feelings about some of them may change and this is okay. You might even discover that what a card means to you in one reading is something completely different to what it tells you in another, and again that's okay. It all depends on what's important at that specific moment in time. –

There are many layers to each card and they hold many meanings.

This book should work for whichever tarot deck you are using, providing it has 78 cards based on the tarot. You might be interested in how other people felt about their cards while doing this exercise – both out of curiosity and as a way to develop. So I am including a few examples of how other people have responded to this exercise too.

Feedback: Exercise 1 Chapter 1

Here's a general mix of feelings that those who have done this first exercise have got from their cards. This demonstrates not only that there is no right answer ... we should all go with our intuition when reading cards .... but to help you learn too, through reading what other people pick up from the images in the cards and seeing them from another person's perspective.

The Empress

• Strong female older wiser a lady .nurturing, earth mother ... get back down to earth .Back to one's roots.

• I like her she is a loving mummy type- woman of power- the power behind the throne- fertility but reversed could mean to be careful of a powerful woman. Upright feel it could be a woman in your life that is a great mentor for you.

• The Empress ... Archangel Gabriel ... I feel abundance from this card. I feel a contentment with what you have and all who draws close to you, I feel you are safe in the knowledge all you need is at your fingertips in the knowing your loved ones, I feel you have a thirst for nurturing and caring for animals and nature, I feel you embrace this along with your love of life and others.

The Hanged Man

• I can see this card would alarm people – has a few meanings from literally hanging around not doing anything about a situation to not doing anything and the outcome will be the same

• Hanged man: hanging from branch angels feet pressing down on forehead: suspension , waiting , only one foot tied … sacrifice …a way out if one wanted .

• Sacrifice(12): giving up things for others, willing to go without, letting go.

Four of Pentacles:

• One angel, one devil, 4 coins two under a male sitting on chair holding a large coin, one other coin situated between angel and devil. - Being possessive materialistic. Greed. Reassurance financial situation. Insecure .

• Four of Discs: Materialism, greedy, material items too important.

• Four of Earth: I feel times are a little difficult right now, you are taking firm control of the purse strings and indeed are reigning in the guide ropes for period of time until you feel able to let them go a little. I feel this is a measure taken to accumulate funds for a project or holiday … something that will indeed benefit and uplift you.

Eight of Cups

• 8 chalices: A man looking through telescope towards the stars in the sky seeking something … truth? Opportunities … answers

• 8 of cups: Another ominous looking card- there is an in-balance of some kind – letting go of the past – moving forward- seeking a better life

• Eight of Cups: Abandonment; feeling left alone, sad, empty, past treasures forgotten, leaving the old for a positive change, abandoning bad habits.

• Eight of Water: I feel a re-evaluation of all things personal is needed. A reshuffle. Is there things you can dispose of allocate to a good cause? I feel you are looking into changing things around. – Out with the old, just less is more sort of thing. I feel this also goes for relationships that have no purpose any more … not any in particular just those you have out grown figuratively speaking.

Interesting responses? I think so and it's quite insightful to compare them as there are many similar responses throughout all cards. What's also interesting about this is each response comes from a different deck of cards yet the different images in the cards are triggering very similar responses.

Exercise Feedback, Chapter 2

As this was a fun exercise, it's fun too, to read how other people have responded. Here are some answers our students have given to this exercise.

0: Fool –

Peter Pan

Forrest Gump (card: the Green Man)

Fools Rush In

Dick Whittington

Nelly the Elephant packed her Trunk and said goodbye to the Circus

1: Magician –

A Midsummer Night's Dream - David Copperfield

Hey Mr. Tambourine Man – Bob Dylan

Professor Snape in Harry Potter- Master of the Dark Arts

2: High Priestess -

Stairway to Heaven by Led Zeppelin - Sylvia Browne

The Nun's Story

Mists of Avalon – Arthurian legends from the perspective of the female characters

Morgaine is taken to Avalon and trained as a priestess of the Mother Goddess. She becomes aware of the rising tension between the old Pagan and new Christian religions. After 7 years she is initiated as a priestess of the Mother and she starts to be groomed as the next Lady of Avalon.

3: Empress –

The Sound of Music

Turning Point – When her daughter joins a ballet company her mother is forced to confront her long ago decision to give up the stage to have a family

Princess Diana

4: Emperor –

Hey Jude, the Beatles – rocky III

Pursuit of Happiness – A man believes in a product he can't sell. Loses his wife, money etc which is an important lesson. His next steps help shape him into the person he next becomes. Against all odds he takes an unpaid internship to become a stockbroker fighting for a single job at the end of it. A powerful story of personal struggles in business.

Dumbledore Harry Potter

5: Heirophant -

Jane Eyre ... sees the unfolding of Jane's moral and spiritual sensibility. As she learns about herself as a student and through experience she also works as a governess. The Hierophant can signify a time of increased study or learning ... someone of authority ... a mentor ... greater spiritual awareness.

Ghandi

Hare Krishna

6: Lovers –

Wuthering Heights ... Cathy torn between her love of Heathcliffe or Edgar and in accepting Edgar's proposal she makes a no turning back choice which effects her relationship with Heathcliffe and the next generation.

City of Angels – An angel, Seth watching over the city finds his job difficult when he falls in love with Maggie. She becomes interested in Seth, and soon his not-quite-mortal state seems a barrier rather than a gift. A choice must be made between celestial duty and earthly love.

The Life of Phi

Richard Burton and Elizabeth Taylor

7: Chariot –

We are the Champions by Queen

Speed – starring Steve McQueen (or was it called bullet) the one where they went up and down the hills in San Francisco

8: Justice –

Robin Hood.

Cinderella.

Wall Street – Every dream has its price. What happens when the desire to succeed takes over your life and you're pushed to your limits and expected to do something you can't do that is illegal and against your moral principles?

9: Hermit –

Robinson Crusoe, shipwrecked on an island during a storm and becomes closer to god, not through attending church but spending time alone with nature with only a bible to read.

Jesus want's you for a sunbeam

10: Wheel of Fortune –

November Rain by Guns n Roses – Manifest your Destiny

The Times They are A-changing Bob Dylan

Blackpool pleasure park and casino

11: Strength

Hercules

A Beautiful Mind

12: Hanged Man –

One Flew Over the Cuckoo's nest

If your'e going to San Francisco be sure to wear some flowers in your hair

13: Death –

The Green Man by Type O Negative

The Carousel film

When you Walk through a Storm, song in the Carousel

14: Temperance

The Mexican Fisherman Story

"Mathematics expresses values that reflect the cosmos, including orderliness, balance, harmony, logic, and abstract beauty." — Deepak Chopra

15: Devil —

The Witches of Eastwick

House of the Rising Sun — The Animals

16: Tower —

Wild World by Cat Stevens (card: the Initiation); the movie the Ice Age

Towering Inferno

17: Star —

Wish upon a Star

Twinkle Twinkle Little Star

18: Moon —

The Call of the Wild ... a book of nature versus nurture ... the two dogs in the moon card. The wild one howling at the moon and the tame one: our tame side.

Dark Night of the Soul

Alice in Wonderland

Beauty and the Beast - don't be fooled by appearances

19: Sun –

Happy by Pharrell –

Snow White and the Seven Dwarves

Oh What a Beautiful Morning song from Oklahoma

Postcards – James Blunt

Sunshine you are my sunshine – you make me happy when skies are blue

20: Judgement –

A Christmas Carol

Disney's Frozen (card: Rebirth)

21: World –

The Time Traveller's wife

Coca Cola Advert – He has the whole World in his hands

Chapter Three Exercise

So far we have had an introduction to tarot cards and how to keep a tarot journal, an introduction to the Minor Arcana and in Lesson Three we looked at the symbolism in the tarot. Exercise for Chapter Three was to choose a tarot card with a character on and to try to get into that character's head and see things from their perspective. Also to choose a tarot card and write a story about the card, its characters, what they might be feeling, planning, experiencing and what lessons they might learn from this.

Remember there are no rights and wrongs when reading the tarot and the most important thing to remember is to trust your intuition. Go with your instincts. However it can help and it is interesting too, to read how other people have responded to this exercise. Here is some of the response received to Lesson Three's Exercise:

6 of Wands: I see a man on a horse sitting looking very proud. This man has a sense of achievement. He has overcome obstacles and has reason to feel good. He deserves the praise and acclaim others are giving him. He is being recognised for his achievements. Once this moment is over he will need to accept the change that comes after reaching the end of the road. If I had to get into his head this is what I'd be thinking: I did this! I came through it all and it's great to be recognised for what I've done. It was worth all the effort. But what do I do now? I need new challenges but at least I now know what I'm capable of.

5 of Pentacles: Two figures are trudging through the snow looking cold and as if they're struggling through life. Almost as if they've got nowhere to go. One is on crutches. The other is clutching at the shawl around his or her neck. This is what I feel this person's feeling: Life is unkind. I'm cold, hungry, tired and sick of it all. How long will I keep struggling like this? Why do I have to go through this when there are others enjoying life and having fun? But there is a light in the window and there was someone who told me to come to them if ever I needed to. So why am I so proud to admit I need their help? If I reach out to them, life could be very different. What have I got to lose?

Strength: Feelings of control, courage, inner belief and self-control as well as compassion for others through love and patience (taming the lion). I feel the Lion represents Leo in the star signs and may have to do with taming the ego. – Real strength comes from within to keep believing without the ego getting in the way; a sort of self-protection and survival instinct. I feel this is a motivating card. The lessons learned through the experiences in this card are mostly strength comes from within ourselves. Do not allow others or situations to get the better of us. It is time to go forward with plans with belief that they will work out.

8 of Pentacles: I am a craftsman. I am working on the eighth pentacle. Seven have already been completed. I have worked hard to learn these skills. I started from the bottom and worked my butt off often doing without but I knew that once I achieved the qualification it would lead to better things. And now it has all been worth it. I'm producing good work. I'm being recognised for my talents. More work is coming in. I'm getting paid for my skills. Life is good. I may even be able to teach other people similar skills. If I had to say what lessons have been learned I would tell everyone to persevere because hard work does bring its just rewards.

High Priestess: I am the High Priestess - I walk the earth draped with robes of silver. I have a silver crescent moon adorning my third eye. I carry a crystal gazing ball in my hand. I stand at a wishing well and have a swan for a companion. The moon is out in the night sky. Flowers are beginning to bud at my feet. I have strong intuition if I look deep within. I am spiritual and connected to my subconscious mind. I urge others to look within themselves too and pay attention for symbolism in their dreams. I guide them to listen to their subconscious to shed light on their obstacles. The moon helps to illuminate that which is remaining hidden. My swan companion is teaching us that knowledge will not come from books or actions but rather listening deep within. Together the Swan and I look into the well with the Moon high above our head. I sense new beginnings and enlightenment. Listening to our intuition will help us with future adversity. The Swan and I will enlighten others to their spiritual side. – Spreading the light. The Moon will guide us on our journey and the well will nourish us, while swan and I walk side by side.

The Moon: Here I am on my own again. I am huddled over feeling cold. It is Twilight but I have hardly noticed the drizzle is slowly soaking me but I hardly feel it. I am too deep in thought remembering past loss and hurts and wallowing in my misery. Staring blankly into the river that flows before me. If I turn my head I will be able to see the moon peeking through the clouds but why would I want to do that? Why would I want to tear my thoughts away from my misery. I have no reason to move forward what if I have a really good day the thoughts come back stabbing me like a knife the wound going deeper every time. I am better off just re-living the past without it sneaking up on me when my guard is down and tearing me apart anew. The pain would be so raw unbearable in fact. Something caught my eye- yes it is the moon all bright and it seems to be smiling at me. Maybe I could try and help myself a little. Maybe I could continue to grieve but not let it be all consuming. Maybe I could take little steps towards putting the past behind me. I would still be standing alone but perhaps just perhaps there are better times ahead for me. Someone once told me that nothing stays the same forever so I could be optimistic that there are better times ahead for me. I won't forget the past but I won't let it rule my future either.

The Chariot: The Chariot is a strong man with a strong mind, he has set is journey and knows where he is heading and nothing will stop him. He has the stars surrounding him and the moon on his shoulders which speaks of power and strength and using his intuition. He has the town behind him and doesn't look back only forward. He holds a wand in one hand which has a small frame which lights his way. The sphinxes are out in front of him and are both white and black which I feel represent the qualities of the man he has both strength and depth and purity and peace and shows that everything in life is a circle and we need both light and darkness to grow as a person. He has both wings and a crest which shows he's grounded but also a highly intuitive person that has far to go.

Chapter Four Exercise

Here is the review of Tarot Lesson Four and examples of other people's responses to this Exercise:

It can help us get a feel for the different cards by taking a certain feature such as a symbol, number or colour and seeing how they compare in the images of the different cards. For Lesson Four I asked that you choose a number and compare this number through the different suits. Here are some of the comparisons received and the different approaches people have taken to this exercise:

I have chosen the number 5

5 represents change - instability – conflict- possible loss-sorrow and misfortune. Cups - Cups represent human feeling-emotion and the power of love or lack of it. Cups represent water signs. 5 of cups: Emotional loss- feelings of sorrow. This card represents the loss of the number 5. Pentacles - Pentacles are associated with Earth signs and represent material wealth-foundations – our talents or lack of them. 5 of Pentacles: There is always something lacking when this card is pulled. Dependent on the other cards in the spread this card represents the instability and misfortune of the number 5. Wands - Wands represent new growth – creativity- passion and initiative – the fire within- Wand represent Fire signs. 5 of Wands: Conflict internal or external – always a lesson learnt from a conflict. This card represents the change and conflict of the number 5. Swords - Swords are action cards – logic and reason – the mind and double edged that can make us disillusioned and things can be deceptive – Swords are Air signs. 5 of Swords: Winning at all costs – somebody else's loss-this card represents the loss conflict and misfortune of the number 5

Cards I picked for this lesson are:

2 swords, 2 wands, 2 cups and 2 of pentacles. Similarities are as follows:

2 of cups and the two of wands, both have two people in picture.

The two pictures that also have pictures of impending storms are 2 of swords and 2 of wands.

2 of swords and 2 of pentacles have very different outlooks in life.

2 of pentacles gives the impression of a new venture in life, where the 2 of swords give the impression of conflict.

In all respect they all have the same going for them in relation to the number 2 i.e. Partnerships duality, balance of opportunities and conflict negotiations. (2 of cups and 2 of swords, both have stormy skies).

I Chose the number two for this Exercise

The twos have underlying themes of partnership, balance, duality, choice and patience.

2 of Wands can bring rewards for past work and putting creative ideas into practice (work and creativity relating to wands). This card tells you to keep believing in yourself and your abilities. Plans already begun could well lead to a successful outcome and the choice could be between taking a risk in order to grow or to remain on familiar ground.

2 of Cups can bring rewards through relationships. A bond of love or friendship is forming. Possibly a reconciliation. A good time to let go of old grievances, to forgive and forget or to work on establishing a new relationship.

2 of Swords can suggest the need to keep the lines of communication open in order to keep partnerships and business relationships balanced. Treating each other as equals can be significant part of the process.

2 of pentacles can relate to balancing finances, balancing a need for material resources with taking time off for self. Perhaps a time to find a balance between friendship, work, family life and relaxation. The more harmonious the balance the happier you will be.

I Chose 8s for this exercise:

Eight of Wands: Action and excitement. Things moving fast but you will be successful. Moving away and adding to your experiences.

Eight of Cups: Time to let go and cut losses, walk away.

Eight of Pentacles: Adding onto skills you have, using your skills to increase your craftsmanship thus leading to rewards.

Eight of swords: Being stuck in a unhappy situation of our own making or that all the resources to get out of an unhappy situation are at our disposal. Need to cut ties.

I Chose the Number Eight, too:

Eight of wands: This suggests that you must move forward and use all at your disposal as you have a lot in your artillery to deal with any issues you may encounter.

Eight of cups: It is a time when you may need to retreat, journey on your own quest as life changes and you may be seeking a deeper understanding of yourself. A time to work on yourself.

Eight of pentacles: You are well able to complete tasks yourself. You are self-sufficient and have the skills to provide for yourself and your loved ones.

Eight of swords: You are not facing something or certain things have been kept from you. You need to see the situation for what it is as then you can make the appropriate decisions.

I chose the number fives which represent conflict and change:

5 of wands tells me of challenges in life. And loss from battles fought.

5 of cups tells me of slowing down. And the need of rest.

5 of Pentacles speaks to me of instability; no money and the need for comfort.

5 of swords telling me of the loss and sorrow of loved ones in battle. And the need of change

Feedback to Chapter Five Exercises:

The Card I pulled is the Eight of Discs.

The picture is of eight discs, seven are carefully crafted while the eighth is blank ready to be worked on.

This card reminds me of my Tarot journey. While I came into this class not being able to read a Tarot card at all, I was given the opportunity to learn. I studied the lessons and completed the homework with care and precision. I dedicated myself to learning the Tarot and in return I have acquired a new skill that I wish to perfect. My long term goal is to use the Tarot to bring light and comfort to others.

ii. My court card is the Queen of wands. I feel she is swift in action and determined in what she does. She is supportive to her family and peers. She is questioning where she should go next with her partner and family on their life journey together. She has a sense of purpose about her that drivers her determination. She is also imaginative and creative.

She has the two of Cups to her North. Suggesting a balance in her relationship, her and her partners love is harmonious and flows between them. The relationship will continue to be successful if the balance continues between them of a give and take relationship.

To her South she has the Two of Discs. Suggesting if they are balanced in their financial situation and work hard it will pay off. There will be loss but it will be replaced with gain as this could be a new career or job opportunity. A continued effort to work towards their goals will see them through any hardships they may face.

To her East is the Six of Wands. Suggesting success on their journey with the hard work they put in. This could be that promotion they were waiting for, or acquired the skills they needed to move further in life, or that someone has noticed and acknowledged the skills they possess. This card also speaks of a harmonious domestic relationship, and her home would be warm and loving , stable and inviting. I feel her connection with her partner and children would be very nurturing and filled with the passion she has for her family.

To her West is the Six of Swords. Suggesting that as things may not have been easy to get where she is or where they are going, it will lighten up and things will seem to better fall into place for them. Keeping a positive attitude through the tough times will help. Any strains that may have occurred due to the situations faced will be eased and find that balance again.

For her Conclusion She has The Lady (3)(The Empress) Suggesting that listening to her intuition and subconscious and working hard acting on her passions and determination, will eventually lead her to the outcome she desires. Things will be full of beauty and pleasure. She may nurture a new idea, or perhaps an addition to the family. (I know we can't comment on Pregnancy though) She will then harvest the fruits of her and her partners labour and commitment they have put in faithfully together.

First set of Two: Queen of Cups and Two of Discs

I feel you it is time to stop and listen to your intuition at this time. How are you feeling about current situations? You may not be moving in the direction you are wanting to go. Being a bit more flexible at work and home may be the key to feel like life is flowing again. Being flexible isn't about letting others take advantage of your kindness either, but rather knowing what you have to do and dealing it out accordingly and evenly. These cards also suggest if you are not happy in your current job situation, it may be time to sit and think about a career change.

Second Set of Two: Death and Ace of Wands

I feel now is a time of rebirth of yourself. Shedding your old skin and starting anew. You may have ideas of projects you would like to tackle in your head. Now would be the ideal time to start on those creative ideas you have been putting aside and break out on your new path with determination and creative energy. One phase of your life will be ending but you have the drive to take the torch and illuminate the new path for you to travel.

Third Set of Two: Page of Cups and Five of Cups

I feel you have been reflecting on a past event that was out of your control and may feel a bit of regret about. As hard as it may be to move on from situations it isn't healthy to dwell on the "What if?" and "why". It is best to take what we can from those situations and move on learning the lessons were taught. Take that knowledge and use it toward future situations to help yourself not be in those situations that you will regret in the end. Look for the beauty in everything even the darkest parts, when the sun goes to sleep the earth does not mourn but rather watches the light show from the heavens above.

****

This brings you to the end of your Tarot Course. I hope you have enjoyed it and feel it has helped you move forward in your understanding of the tarot.

Thank you for taking this journey with me.

Made in the USA
Coppell, TX
18 February 2023